Pelican Books
Introducing Shakespeare

Dr G. B. Harrison, Emeritus Professor of English in the University of Michigan, was born in 1894. He went up to Queens' College, Cambridge, as a Classical Exhibitioner in 1913. In the First World War he served in the Queen's Royal Regiment from 1914 to 1919 in India and Mesopotamia. In 1919 he went back to Cambridge and studied English Literature, specializing in the Elizabethan period. He was for many years Reader in English Literature in the University of London. In the Second World War he returned to the Army and served in the R.A.S.C. and the Intelligence Corps. In 1943 he was released from the Army to go to Canada to take up the position of Head of the Department of English at Queen's University. In 1949 he became Professor of English at the University of Michigan until his retirement from active teaching in 1963. His best-known works are the five volumes of *Elizabethan* and *Jacobean Journals* in which he traces from day to day those events, great and small, which excited Shakespeare and his contemporaries. He is author of *Shakespeare at Work*, *The Life and Death of Robert Devereux, Earl of Essex*, *Elizabethan Plays and Players*, and editor of The Bodley Head Quartos, Penguin Shakespeare, and many other works.

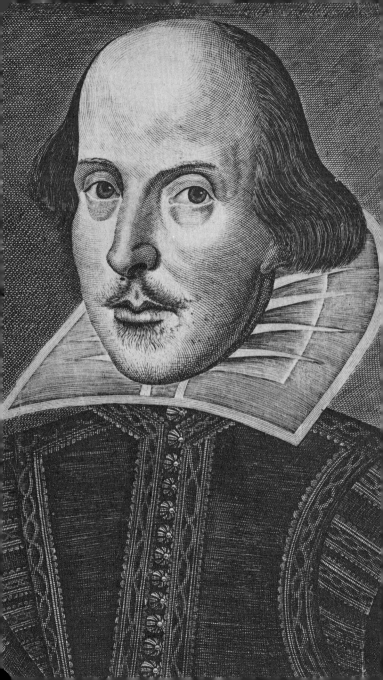

G. B. Harrison

Introducing Shakespeare

Third Edition: revised and expanded

Penguin Books

Penguin Books Ltd, Harmondsworth,
Middlesex, England
Penguin Books Inc., 7110 Ambassador Road,
Baltimore, Maryland 21207, U.S.A.
Penguin Books Australia Ltd, Ringwood,
Victoria, Australia

First published 1939
Reprinted 1941, 1948
Revised edition 1954
Reprinted 1957, 1959, 1962, 1963
Third edition (revised and expanded) 1966
Reprinted 1968, 1971

Made and printed in Great Britain by
Hazell Watson & Viney Ltd, Aylesbury, Bucks
Set in Times New Roman

Contents

MAR   1987

List of Plates

Acknowledgements

To the British Museum for the following extracts from *Hamlet*, v, i (pp. 209–13): A, B, D and E; to the Cambridge University Press and the British Museum for extract F (p. 213); to the Folger Museum, Washington D.C., for extract C (p. 210).

Preface

Introducing Shakespeare was originally put together during the Munich crisis of 1938 and first published in the spring of 1939. Since that time so much has been written about Shakespeare, his times, his theatre, and his texts that a complete revision is now needed. The original book has therefore been rewritten and much expanded. *Introducing Shakespeare* is intended for the use of the general reader who needs some kind of aid in a first understanding of Shakespeare, and partly also as a general introduction to the Penguin Shakespeares. In the expanded version, I have added a new chapter on Shakespeare's Age. On the other hand I have not considered modern Shakespearean criticism, which is now so varied and voluminous that no brief treatment is possible.

Quotations from the plays are from the Penguin Shakespeares. In printing extracts from ancient records, the spelling has been modernized except in a few instances where the original spelling seemed to have significance.

I would express my thanks to those who have criticized the original version. And I am especially grateful to Mr C. Walter Hodges for permission to use his reconstructions of the Elizabethan stage.

G.B.H.

1

Shakespeare's Fame

No household in the English-speaking world is properly furnished unless it contains copies of the *Holy Bible* and of *The Works of William Shakespeare*. It is not always thought necessary that these books should be read in maturer years, but they must be present as symbols of Religion and Culture.

Shakespeare has not always been so symbolic a figure. He was once an actor and a playwright, when neither actors nor stage-plays were regarded as respectable or of any importance. The notion that he was the supreme Genius of the English-Speaking Races did not begin until he had been dead more than a century: but since then it has become so firmly accepted that no schoolboy can avoid a detailed study of at least one of his plays.

Nevertheless, the first public notice of Shakespeare was hostile and unkind. In the autumn of 1592, Robert Greene, the most popular author of his generation, lay penniless and dying. Greene was a Cambridge man who had written several successful plays. The players had grown rich on the products of his brain, and now he was deserted and alone. He wrote a letter to three of his friends who had likewise helped to make the fortunes of the players, warning them to avoid his misfortunes. 'Is it not strange, that I, to whom they all have been beholding, is it not like that you to whom they all have been beholding, shall (were ye in that case as I am now) be both at once of them forsaken?' There was a among his priuate friends,&c.

As *Plautus* and *Seneca* are accounted
the best for Comedy and Tragedy among
the Latines : so *Shakespeare* among ÿ English is the most excellent in both kinds for
the stage;for Comedy, witnes his *Gētlemē*
of Verona,his *Errors*,his *Loue labors lost*,his
Loue labours wonne,his *Midsummers night*
dreame,& his *Merchant of Venice*:for Tragedy his *Richard the 2.Richard the 3.Hen-*
ry the 4.King Iohn,*Titus Andronicus* and
his *Romeo* and *Iuliet*.

As *Epius Stolo* said,that the Muses would
speake with *Plautus* tongue,if they would
speak Latin:so I say that the Muses would
speake with *Shakespeares* fine filed phrase,if
they would speake English.

As *Musæus*,who wrote the loue of *Hero*
and *Leander*,had two excellent schollers,
Thamaras & *Hercules*:so hath he in England two excellent Poets,imitators of him
in the same argument and subiect,*Christo-*
pher Marlow,and *George Chapman*.

As *Ouid* saith of his worke;

> *Iamqȝ opus exegi,quod nec Iouis ira,nec ignis,*
> *Nec poteris ferrum,nec edax abolere vetustas.*

And as *Horace* saith of his;*Exegi monum-*
mentū ære perennius;Regaliqȝ situ pyramidū
altius;Quod non imber edax; Non Aquilo
impotens possit diruere; aut innumerabilis

amorum

1 A page from Francis Meres's *Palladis Tamia*, 1598

greater grievance. 'Yes, trust them not,' Greene went on, 'for there is an upstart Crow, beautified with our feathers, that with his *Tiger's heart wrapt in a Player's hide*,* supposes he is as well able to bombast out a blank verse as the best of you: and being an absolute *Johannes factotum*, is in his own conceit the only Shake-scene in a country.'

At this time Shakespeare was only a beginner. The *Henry the Sixth* plays, particularly the First Part (which was first produced in March 1592) achieved considerable success, but none of the plays which made him famous had yet been written.

Six years later, in 1598, an earnest young student named Francis Meres produced a book called *Palladis Tamia*, an elaborate volume of what he called 'Similitudes'. It was an anthology of specimens of fine writing culled from more than a hundred and fifty authors. To this he added a chapter entitled 'A Comparative Discourse of our English poets with the Greek, Latin, and Italian poets.' Shakespeare was easily his favourite amongst English authors, praised as one of eight by whom 'the English tongue is mightily enriched, and gorgeously invested in rare ornaments and resplendent habiliments.' He was one of six who had raised *monumentum aere perennius*; one of five who excelled in lyric poetry; one of thirteen 'our best for tragedy'; one of seventeen 'best for comedy'. Moreover, Meres picked him out for special mention, not given to the others:

As the soul of Euphorbus was thought to live in Pythagoras: so the sweet witty soul of Ovid lives in mellifluous and honey-tongued Shakespeare, witness his *Venus and Adonis*, his *Lucrece*, his sugared Sonnets among his private friends, &c.

As Plautus and Seneca are accounted the best for Comedy and Tragedy among the Latins: so Shakespeare among the English is the most excellent in both kinds for the stage. For Comedy, witness his *Gentlemen of Verona*, his *Errors*, his *Love's Labour's Lost*, his *Love's*

* A parody of a striking line in *III Henry VI* (I, iv, 137) – 'Oh tiger's heart wrapp'd in a woman's hide.'

*Labour Won,** his *Midsummer Night's Dream*, and his *Merchant of Venice*; for Tragedy, his *Richard the 2*, *Richard the 3*, *Henry the 4*, *King John*, *Titus Andronicus* and his *Romeo and Juliet*.

As Epius Stolo said, that the Muses would speak with Plautus' tongue, if they would speak Latin; so I say that the Muses would speak with Shakespeare's fine filed phrase, if they would speak English. (See Pl. 1.)

Fourteen years later Shakespeare, now one of the older generation of dramatists, had lost something of his popularity. When John Webster published his play *The White Devil* (1612) he wrote a preface in which, by the way, he praised

that full and heightened style of Master Chapman, the laboured and understanding works of Master Jonson, the no less worthy composures of the both worthily excellent Master Beaumont and Master Fletcher, and lastly (without wrong last to be named) the right happy and copious industry of M. Shakespeare, M. Dekker, and M. Heywood.

In 1623 (seven years after Shakespeare's death), appeared the First Folio – the first collection of his plays in one volume. It was prefaced by various tributes in verse, including a full-dress memorial Ode by Ben Jonson, magnificently superlative. In his private conversation Jonson was more critical. In the *Discoveries*, a collection of notes and jottings, posthumously published in 1641, he recorded:

I remember, the Players have often mentioned it as an honour to Shakespeare, that in his writing, (whatsoever he penned) he never blotted out line. My answer hath been, Would he had blotted a thousand. Which they thought a malevolent speech. I had not told posterity this, but for their ignorance, who choose that circumstance to commend their friend by, wherein he most faulted. And to justify mine own candour, (for I loved the man, and do honour his memory (on this side Idolatry) as much as any). He was (indeed) honest, and of an open, and free nature: had an excellent phantasy; brave notions, and gentle

* *Love's Labour Won* – unless another title for an existing play – has been lost.

expressions: wherein he flowed with that facility, that sometime it was necessary he should be stopped: *Sufflaminandus erat*; as Augustus said of Haterius. His wit was in his own power; would the rule of it had been so too. Many times he fell into those things, could not escape laughter: As when he said in the person of Caesar, one speaking to him; *Caesar, thou dost me wrong*. He replied: *Caesar did never wrong, but with just cause*: and such like; which were ridiculous. But he redeemed his vices, with his virtues. There was ever more in him to be praised, than to be pardoned.

In *Julius Caesar*, the passage as printed in the First Folio reads:

> Know, Caesar doth not wrong, nor without cause
> Will he be satisfied.

Either Jonson misquoted, or more probably Shakespeare heeded Jonson's censure.

In 1668 Dryden published his famous critical dialogue, the *Essay of Dramatic Poesy*. Shakespeare had now been dead fifty-two years, and during this time a second and a third edition of the Folio appeared. He was no longer a modern but not yet a classic whose perennial quality was finally established. Dryden's estimate, expressed in the dialogue, was:

To begin then with Shakespeare; he was the man who of all Modern and perhaps Ancient Poets, had the largest and most comprehensive soul. All the Images of Nature were still present to him, and he drew them not laboriously, but luckily: when he describes any thing, you more than see it, you feel it too. Those who accuse him to have wanted learning, give him the greater commendation: he was naturally learned; he needed not the spectacles of Books to read Nature: he looked inwards, and found her there. I cannot say he is everywhere alike; were he so, I should do him injury to compare him with the greatest of Mankind. He is many times flat, insipid; his Comic wit degenerating into clenches, his serious swelling into Bombast. But he is always great, when some great occasion is presented to him: no man can say he ever had a fit subject for his wit, and did not then raise himself as high above the rest of Poets,

Quantum lenta solent inter viburna cupressi.

The consideration of this made Mr Hales of Eton say, That there was no subject of which any Poet ever writ, but he would produce it much treated of in Shakespeare; and however others are now generally preferred before him, yet the Age wherein he lived, which had contemporaries with him Fletcher and Jonson, never equalled them to him in their esteem: And in the last King's Court, when Ben's reputation was at its highest, Sir John Suckling, and with him the greater part of the Courtiers, set our Shakespeare far above him.

Forty-one years later – in 1709 – Shakespeare was at length established as a classic when Nicholas Rowe, a Restoration dramatist, brought out the first edited collection of his plays. Shakespeare was now sufficiently ancient for the public to need some information about him, and the taste of readers of plays had grown so much nicer that the earlier and simpler methods of printing were unacceptable. Rowe added to his edition a short biographical introduction and some commendations of the passages which he most admired. He also considerably revised the text, adding place headings to the scenes and new stage directions. He was largely responsible for the form in which Shakespeare's plays are normally printed.

After Rowe, complete editions of the plays followed each other quickly, the most famous being those by Alexander Pope, 1723–5; Theobald, 1733; Hanmer, 1743–4; Dr Johnson, 1765; Edmund Malone, 1790. Between 1709 and 1799 no less than sixty editions of the plays, of all kinds including reprints, appeared.

During this century Shakespeare's reputation rapidly increased. Pope, though he was severe on Shakespeare's delinquencies – as he regarded them – was enthusiastic:

If ever any Author deserved the name of an Original, it was Shakespear. Homer himself drew not his art so immediately from the fountains of Nature, it proceeded through Egyptian strainers and channels, and came to him not without some tincture of the learning, or some cast of the models, of those before him. The Poetry of Shakespear was Inspiration indeed : he is not so much an Imitator, as an Instrument, of Nature ; and 'tis not so just to say that he speaks from her, as that she speaks through him.

His Characters are so much Nature her self, that 'tis sort of injury to call them by so distant a name as Copies of her. Those of other Poets have a constant resemblance, which shows that they received them from one another, and were but multipliers of the same image : each picture like a mock-rainbow is but the reflection of a reflection. But every single character in Shakespear is as much an Individual, as those in Life itself ; it is as impossible to find any two alike ; and such as from their relation or affinity in any respect appear most to be Twins, will upon comparison be found remarkably distinct. To this life and variety of Character, we must add the wonderful Preservation of it ; which is such throughout his plays, that had all the Speeches been printed without the very names of the Persons, I believe one might have applied them with certainty to every speaker.

The Power over our Passions was never possessed in a more eminent degree, or displayed in so different instances. Yet all along, there is seen no labour, no pains to raise them ; no preparation to guide our guess to the effect, or be perceived to lead toward it ; But the heart swells, and the tears burst out, just at the proper places ; We are surprised, the moment we weep : and yet upon reflection find the passion so just, that we should be surprised if we had not wept, and wept at that very moment.

Dr Johnson wrote his famous Preface to Shakespeare in 1765. Johnson never praised extravagantly, and he criticized freely. Shakespeare by this time was indisputably a classic, or as Johnson sonorously put it –

The Poet, of whose works I have undertaken the revision, may now begin to assume the dignity of an ancient, and claim the privilege of established fame and prescriptive veneration. He has long outlived his century, the term commonly fixed as the test of literary merit. Whatever advantages he might once derive from personal allusions, local customs, or temporary opinions, have for many years been lost; and every topic of merriment or motive of sorrow, which the modes of artificial life afforded him, now only obscure the scenes which they once illuminated. The effects of favour and competition are at an end; the tradition of his friendships and his enmities has perished; his works support no opinion with arguments, nor supply any faction with invectives; they can neither indulge vanity nor gratify malignity, but are read without any other reason than the desire of pleasure, and are therefore praised only as pleasure is obtained; yet, thus unassisted by interest or passion, they have passed through variations of taste and changes of manners, and, as they devolved from one generation to another, have received new honours at every transmission.

But because human judgement, though it be gradually gaining upon certainty, never becomes infallible; and approbation, though long continued, may yet be only the approbation of prejudice or fashion; it is proper to inquire, by what peculiarities of excellence Shakespeare has gained and kept the favour of his countrymen.

Nothing can please many, and please long, but just representations of general nature. Particular manners can be known to few, and therefore few only can judge how nearly they are copied. The irregular combinations of fanciful invention may delight awhile, by that novelty of which the common satiety of life sends us all in quest; but the pleasures of sudden wonder are soon exhausted, and the mind can only repose on the stability of truth.

Shakespeare is above all writers, at least above all modern writers, the poet of nature: the poet that holds up to his readers a faithful mirror of manners and of life. His characters are not modified by the customs of particular places, unpractised by the rest of the world; by the peculiarities of studies or professions, which can operate but upon small numbers; or by the accidents of transient fashions or temporary opinions: they are the genuine progeny of common humanity, such as the world will always supply, and observation will always find. His persons act and speak by the influence of those general passions and principles by which all minds are agitated, and the whole system of life is continued in motion. In the writings of other poets a character is too often an individual; in those of Shakespeare it is commonly a species.

Meanwhile the cause of the deification of Shakespeare was much advanced. In September 1769, David Garrick, the greatest English actor of the century, organized a three-day celebration at Stratford-on-Avon whereat Shakespeare's memory was honoured by the shooting of cannons, ringing of bells, fireworks, a grand procession, a fancy dress ball, and much oratory. A rotunda was specially constructed in a meadow on the banks of the Avon, and here before a fashionable audience of two thousand persons Garrick declaimed the Ode specially written for the occasion. This was the supreme moment in the celebration which otherwise was a disaster, for the organizers failed to allow for the weather. The rain poured down hour after hour. The roof of the rotunda leaked. The Avon overflowed her banks, and before the end the rotunda and its distinguished company were isolated in the flood. Garrick lost over £2,000, but when he returned to London he produced in Drury Lane Theatre a satirical dramatization called *The Jubilee* which ran for more than ninety performances. Garrick's *Jubilee* was in fact largely responsible for the cult of Shakespeare which has since become so profitable to the citizens of Stratford-on-Avon.

Critics also were becoming infected with the growing enthusiasm. In 1777 Maurice Morgann wrote an *Essay on the Dramatic Character of Sir John Falstaff*. Morgann was not interested in rules or dramatic propriety or Shakespeare's skill (or lack of it). To him Falstaff was a real man whose character and actions should be seriously analysed, and he set out to vindicate Sir John from the charge of cowardice.

By 1790 the learned critics, sage or pedantic, had said all that could then be said about Shakespeare. It was the turn of the scholars. Of these the most important were George Stevens and Edmund Malone. Stevens as early as 1766 realized that the text of Shakespeare had lost as well as gained by the reforming zeal of editors. He therefore reprinted twenty plays from the original Quartos.* Malone, recognizing that the customs of the theatre had changed considerably in two centuries, wrote a historical account of the English stage which was not superseded for nearly a century.

With the turn of the century, and that revolution of interest not always very happily called the Romantic Revival, criticism of Shakespeare changed its tone. Shakespeare was no longer a great English dramatist, a faulty genius; he grew into a godlike figure. Samuel Taylor Coleridge was principally responsible for this conception.

Assuredly [he proclaimed in a lecture] that criticism of Shakspeare will alone be genial which is reverential. The Englishman, who without reverence, a proud and affectionate reverence, can utter the name of William Shakspeare, stands disqualified for the office of critic. He wants one at least of the very senses, the language of which he is to employ, and will discourse at best, but as a blind man, while the whole harmonious creation of light and shade with all its subtle interchange of deepening and dissolving colours rises in silence to the silent *fiat* of the uprising Apollo. However inferior in ability I may be to some who have followed me, I own I am proud that I was the first in time who publicly demonstrated to the full extent of the position, that the supposed irregularity and extravagances of Shakspeare were the mere dreams of a pedantry that arraigned the eagle because it had not the dimensions of the swan. In all the successive courses of lectures delivered by me, since my first attempt at the Royal Institution, it has been, and it still remains, my object, to prove that in all points from the most important to the most minute, the judgement of Shakspeare is commensurate with his genius – nay, that his genius reveals itself in his judgement, as in its most exalted form. And the more gladly do I recur to this subject from the clear conviction, that to judge aright, and with distinct consciousness of the grounds of our judgement, concerning the works of Shakspeare, implies the power and the means of judging rightly of all other works of intellect, those of abstract science alone excepted.

* For Quartos and Folio, see pp. 206–7.

For a century after Coleridge it was still the fashion for those who spoke of Shakespeare in public to adopt the hushed tone and heightened phrases appropriate to a religious occasion.

To Coleridge Shakespeare was not so much a writer of plays as an emanation of the Godhead. Not much had been added to the knowledge of Shakespeare's biography since Rowe's day, and critics, romantically inclined, created their own image of a suitable Shakespeare. To Thomas Carlyle, in his quest for Heroes, Shakespeare was the Peasant Who Became a Prophet.

Whoever looks intelligently at this Shakspeare may recognize that he too was a *Prophet*, in his way; of an insight analogous to the Prophetic, though he took it up in another strain. Nature seemed to this man also divine; *un*speakable, deep as Tophet, high as Heaven; 'We are such stuff as Dreams are made of!' That scroll in Westminster Abbey, which few read with understanding, is of the depth of any Seer. . . .

Well: this is our poor Warwickshire Peasant, who rose to be Manager of a Playhouse, so that he could live without begging; whom the Earl of Southampton cast some kind glances on; whom Sir Thomas Lucy, many thanks to him, was for sending to the Treadmill! We did not account him a god, like Odin, while he dwelt with us; – on which point there were much to be said. But I will say rather, or repeat: In spite of the sad state Hero-worship now lies in, consider what this Shakspeare has actually become among us. Which Englishman we ever made, in this land of ours, which million of Englishmen, would we not give up rather than the Stratford Peasant? There is no regiment of highest Dignitaries that we would sell him for. He is the grandest thing we have yet done. For our honour among foreign nations, as an ornament to our English Household, what item is there that we would not surrender rather than him? Consider now, if they asked us, Will you give up your Indian Empire or your Shakspeare, you English; never have had any Indian Empire, or never have had any Shakspeare? Really it were a grave question. Official persons would answer doubtless in official language; but we, for our part too, should not we be forced to answer: Indian Empire, or no Indian Empire; we cannot do without

Shakspeare! Indian Empire will go, at any rate, some day; but this Shakspeare does not go, he lasts forever with us; we cannot give up our Shakspeare!

This was written in 1840.

By 1875 the Great Figure had declined somewhat in stature. He was still romantic, but at least human. Scholars had been at work on Shakespeare's plays and the order of their writing was fairly accurately established. In *Shakespere, His Mind and Art*, Edward Dowden made popular the notion that Shakespeare's plays show the development of his personality and reflect his private emotional life.

By the end of the century new materials for reconstructing Shakespeare's biography had accumulated, and were assembled in the *Life of William Shakespeare* by Sidney Lee, which for thirty years was regarded as the official biography. Lee had no romantic notions. He refused to believe that the personality of Shakespeare could be deduced from his works, and so, falling back on external facts of biography, he concluded that Shakespeare was a fine specimen of the Industrious Boy Who Got On.

Lee's *Life of Shakespeare* first appeared in 1898. It was often reprinted and enlarged until it became a portly, impressive volume; but the critical reader on closer study found that many of his pronouncements were not statements of proved fact but guesses. After a while an acute scepticism developed when on page after page confident statements were qualified with 'there is little room for doubt', 'it was doubtless', 'it is possible'. Hence there arose a reaction against all biographies of Shakespeare and a general feeling that, after all, nothing was really known about him.

Lee's *Life* was superseded in 1930 by E. K. Chambers' two volumes, *William Shakespeare: A Study of Facts and Problems*. This work was not so much a biography, as a monumental collection of every document, fact, and legend connected with Shakespeare, and, with its four-volume predecessor, *The Elizabethan Stage*, gave students a set of invaluable reference books.

Since 1930, except for Leslie Hotson's tantalizing discovery (see p. 59), few new facts of importance have been added, but many fresh 'approaches' and 'interpretations' have been offered. Some are purely critical, and concerned solely with the plays and their interpretation, but many are part critical, part psychological, interpretations as much of Shakespeare the man as of his plays.

In the 1920s critics of Shakespeare were much affected by the new interest in the Elizabethan theatre. His plays were now regarded less as masterpieces of universal wisdom than as works to be performed in the peculiar conditions of the Globe playhouse.

Of critics of this kind, by far the most important was Harley Granville-Barker. Granville-Barker was uniquely equipped to write about Shakespeare the dramatist. Early in the century as a young professional actor he made his name in some of Shaw's comedies; he wrote successful plays; and in 1911–13 he directed London productions of *The Winter's Tale*, *A Midsummer Night's Dream*, and *Twelfth Night* which revolutionized the staging of Shakespeare's plays for a generation. Before that time a Shakespearean play was usually staged with elaborate scenery and an almost ritualistic kind of acting and diction, while the text was cut and rearranged to suit the performance. Barker substituted a simple but beautiful set so designed that the plays were acted rapidly and without cuts or alterations; and he insisted that his actors bring out the full effect of the poetry and the meaning of every word.

In the 1920s Barker turned critic and began a series of *Prefaces* in each of which he studied a single play as a work to be produced on the stage – its total effect, the nature of the characters and the interpretation of the part, the texture of the poetry, and the harmony of the whole production. He thus stressed Shakespeare the practical man of the theatre. Granville-Barker's ten *Prefaces* are a rare combination of scholarship, intimate knowledge of the theatre and the actor's profession, and artistic intuition.

Other developments followed. In the 1930s there was a new zeal for a close and detailed study of Shakespeare's actual poetic technique. It varied from the elaborate card-indexing of Shakespeare's poetic imagery adopted by Caroline Spurgeon in *Shakespeare's Imagery* (1934) to the personal and subjective essays of G. Wilson Knight in *The Wheel of Fire*, *The Imperial Theme*, and other volumes, a process which he calls 'interpretation'.

This kind of study is primarily concerned with style as a revelation of personality. Great poets are individuals both in personality and in expression. Poetic style consists – apart from the content – largely of individual rhythms, and more particularly of an individual use of myths, symbols, and images (which used to be called 'metaphors' and 'similes'). A poet's metaphors spring from his personality and experience. A bookish poet, such as Milton or Pope, draws most of his images from the books that he has read: he and his readers take an acute pleasure in these literary echoes. Less learned and more original poets use images which spring from their own personal experiences or, to quote Caroline Spurgeon, the poet

may be, and in Shakespeare's case is, almost entirely objective in his dramatic characters and their views and opinions, yet, like the man who under stress of emotion will show no sign of it in eye or face, but will reveal it in some muscular tension, the poet unwittingly lays bare his own innermost likes and dislikes, observations and interests, associations of thought, attitudes of mind and beliefs, in and through the images, the verbal pictures he draws to illuminate something quite different in the speech and thought of his characters.

Caroline Spurgeon sought to display Shakespeare's personality and her method was to card-index, analyse, and tabulate all Shakespeare's images, and, as part of the process, to analyse the imagery used by other Elizabethan dramatists. The result was to confirm certain impressions: that Shakespeare has far more images drawn from sport than other dramatists, that Marlowe's imagery is predominantly drawn from the classics, and so forth.

It is a fascinating pastime, and one of the few forms of literary research that can be carried out at home. One requires only a volume of Shakespeare's plays and a number of cards for the card-index.

The values and limitations of this kind of study lie in its being objective. An absolutely mechanical scientific collection of such statistics reveals many of the processes of the human mind which would escape notice altogether in ordinary reading. It cannot be carried too far, for a poetic image is not a simple or mechanical expression but, especially in Shakespeare's later period, a fusion of all kinds of sparkling ideas. Often it is quite impossible to separate the particular images in a clot of images such as:

> Come thick Night,
> And pall thee in the dunnest smoke of Hell,
> That my keen knife see not the wound it makes,
> Nor Heaven peep through the blanket of the dark,
> To cry, hold, hold.

In this passage neither *knife* nor *blanket* can suitably be classified under 'Images drawn from domestic articles'.

Nevertheless, within reason, a study of imagery gives results similar to chemical analysis. A study of Shakespeare's imagery reveals many of his experiences, but not how and when he came by them.

Occasionally, when the material exists, it is possible to trace the actual source of a poetic image. J. Livingston Lowes studied Coleridge's *Kubla Khan* and *The Ancient Mariner*. As external evidence he had Coleridge's notebooks, which showed what Coleridge had been reading at the time. Moreover, from Dorothy Wordsworth's *Journals* and similar sources, Coleridge's external experiences were recorded. As a result, in *The Road to Xanadu*, Lowes was able to trace back almost every idea and phrase in *Kubla Khan* and *The Ancient Mariner* to its original source, and thereby to present a fascinating picture of a poet's mind and how it worked. Similarly, by comparing Keats' letters and his poetry, J. Middleton Murry was able to show how Keats' mind worked.

Unfortunately there are no notebooks for Shakespeare, and any deductions must be largely guesswork. One cannot even tell whether an image is negative or positive. A man may be full of images of sport either because he is himself a great sportsman, or because he is feeble-bodied and admires those of better physique. Sports writers are not necessarily expert sportsmen. Nor are those who make a particular study of Shakespeare's imagery agreed amongst themselves.

Once, having a private theory of my own, based on the fact that Shakespeare's images drawn from the sea and war indicated that at some time or other he had seen war and the sea at first hand, I put it to two authorities* on Shakespearean imagery. I asked each of them the same question: 'Do you, from your intensive study of Shakespeare's imagery, gather that he had personal experience of the sea?' The one replied, 'Of course'; and the other, 'Certainly not'.

From this one can deduce that, just as a poetic image comes from a poet's experience, which includes the books that he has read, so also the perception of an image and of its significance by readers or hearers comes from their experience. Unless the critic has known the same kind of experiences as the author he will miss many images and their significance. Miss Spurgeon, for instance, was unaware of many of the images recorded in Eric Partridge's *Shakespeare's Bawdy*. As Keats put it in a letter, when writing of Wordsworth: 'We find what he says true as far as we have experienced, and we can judge no further but by larger experience – for axioms in philosophy are not axioms until they are proved upon our pulses. We read fine things, but never feel them to the full until we have gone the same steps as the author – I know this is not plain; you will know exactly my meaning

* G. Wilson Knight and Caroline Spurgeon.

when I say that now I shall relish Hamlet more than I have ever done.'

In this kind of interpretation scholarship is important, for until the reader himself has some knowledge of Elizabethan idiom – and this requires a considerable knowledge of the Elizabethan background – he cannot appreciate the full meaning of many Elizabethan images. Macbeth, for instance, returning from the murder of Duncan with his hands covered with blood, and dazed with horror at what he has seen and done, murmurs:

> One cried God bless us, and Amen the other,
> As they had seen me with these hangman's hands.

To a modern reader there is no reason why a hangman should have unclean hands; it would show a lack of delicacy for him to exercise his sordid profession unwashed. But to Shakespeare's audience the phrase has a ghastly significance; in executions for treason – and there had been several just before *Macbeth* was written – it was the hangman's business to tear out the victim's entrails before hacking the body into quarters.

From her collections of images, Caroline Spurgeon was also able to demonstrate that 'clusters' of significant images appear in different plays; *Hamlet* is full of images of ulcers and diseases, *Romeo and Juliet* of images of light, *Macbeth* of images of clothing, ill-fitting and stolen, as if Macbeth had assumed garments which were too big for him.

To a scientifically minded generation these discoveries were exciting. Here, at first sight, had appeared a method of examining the plays and the mental processes of this author which was objective, and based on verifiable evidence. Critics, steeped in the newer psychological methods which ultimately derived from the psychoanalytic school of Sigmund Freud, proceeded to demonstrate all kinds of subconscious symbols, significances, and patterns of thought and expression which would reveal Shakespeare's soul. In this kind of examination, one of the most successful was

R. B. Heilman's *This Great Stage* (1948), an elaborate study of the 'patterns' in *King Lear*.

Shakespeare's plays were thus once more removed from the Elizabethan stage and brought back into the library (and the laboratory), for this intricate relationship of images and ideas can only be perceived in leisurely study. Shakespeare the poet and philosopher was once more exalted while Shakespeare the practical actor-playwright was ignored. If Shakespeare was himself aware of the patterns of imagery which his modern critics have discovered, and deliberately used such symbolism as part of the dramatic structure of his plays, it follows that the more intelligent members of his audiences must have been acutely sensitive, for it is not easy to perceive such subtleties when watching a play wherein the words are spoken rapidly and the action is quick, vivid, and noisy. If so, it should increase our respect for the intelligence of the Elizabethan theatre-goers.

In the last thirty years there has been such a mass of critical writing* that no short account can be given of individual works, but the general reader can find guidance in the annual summaries of the new work given in *The Shakespeare Survey*. Nor need he be depressed at the thought that to read Shakespeare's plays he must first study a thousand works of scholarship and criticism. Indeed, he will be best advised to begin by ignoring everything but the play itself. Only when he is entirely familiar with a play can he find enlightenment in a critic. Later, his understanding and delight may be increased by more specialized study, for modern scholarship and criticism have become an affair for experts. *Introducing Shakespeare* aims rather at giving that minimum of preparation which will help him towards an enjoyable first reading.

* For the year 1965 alone the annual bibliography in *The Shakespeare Quarterly* recorded 1,807 items.

2

Materials for the Life of Shakespeare

To those who have never studied Elizabethan records at first hand it may seem surprising and mysterious that there should be a dearth of intimate information about Shakespeare: so famous an Englishman, and such an unsatisfactory biography! Yet there is no mystery, for even in the lives of the greatest and most spectacular persons of the time there are many gaps.

There have been many lives of Queen Elizabeth I, each giving a somewhat different or even contradictory interpretation; but two of the most important facts about her are unknown or disputable. She was certainly the daughter of the Lady Anne Boleyn; but was her father Henry VIII (as is generally believed), or was he – as her sister Mary declared – Mark Smeaton, the musician who was afterwards executed on the charge of committing adultery with the Lady Anne? And again, was Elizabeth indeed the Virgin Queen? or was she, as Ben Jonson gossiped with William Drummond, one who tried many men for her pleasure? Unless there is a certain answer to such questions, any attempt to write a biography must in part at least be conjecture or historical fiction.

Nowadays it is easy to compile the biography of a modern dramatist. The essential facts of his life, his birth, his progress at school, at the university, and elsewhere, his marriage, and his death, are available in public records. While he is alive a number of the facts of his life are given in *Who's Who*. His plays, as they come out, are noticed in newspapers and periodicals, and a little research in the files shows when the run of any particular play began and ended. He writes letters, which are carefully preserved, for the letters of eminent authors are commercially valuable. When he dies journalists and critics hasten to write obituary notices and to record their impressions of his personality. Enough material is thus provided for anyone to write quite a considerable Life.

Little of this material remains for the biographer of dramatists of the seventeenth century. The parish registers record the dates of baptism, marriage, and burial, but many of the registers are lost. There were no newspapers, very few diaries, and few individuals wrote chatty letters. Players and dramatists were regarded as persons of dubious standing, about whom no one was likely to be much interested unless they were concerned with some scandal or were made the victims of some scurrilous joke.

Moreover, literary persons are seldom spectacular. The man who leads a life of heroic action has neither the time, nor usually the desire, to express himself in writing. Those who gallop down valleys of death seldom sing about their experiences; they leave it to poets living placidly in country rectories or suburban lodgings to write glorious and heroic ballads, as *The Charge of the Light Brigade*, or *Ye Mariners of England*. To be a great writer a man must spend much of his time at a table in the laborious act of writing, which is neither an exciting nor a spectacular occupation. Unless a writer of former days leaves a diary, or (like Keats) writes many letters which his friends keep, or attracts a biographer (as Dr Johnson attracted Boswell), or meets a note-taker (as Ben Jonson met William Drummond of Hawthornden), or (like Christopher Marlowe) is in trouble with the authorities, the interesting details of his life vanish as soon as those who knew him die. Even today, when a literary man has news value, most

2 Martin Droeshout's engraving of Shakespeare. The earliest known states; from a copy of the First Folio

Mr. WILLIAM

SHAKESPEARES

COMEDIES,
HISTORIES, &
TRAGEDIES.

Published according to the True Originall Copies:

Martin Droeshout sculpsit London.

LONDON
Printed by Isaac Iaggard, and Ed. Blount. 1623.

of his readers know little more of him than can be amply contained on a postcard.

There is a special difficulty in trying to write a life of Shakespeare. For the past hundred years and more a belief has been expressed by various enthusiasts that Shakespeare's plays were not really written by William Shakespeare but by Francis Bacon, or by Christopher Marlowe, or by Edward de Vere, Earl of Oxford, or by Queen Elizabeth, or by William Stanley, Earl of Derby, or by some other. These agnostics usually call themselves 'Anti-Stratfordians'. It is, however, a fact that so far no reputable scholar with first-hand knowledge of the Elizabethan Age and its literature has ever supported the claim; but the argument has long been so highly charged with emotion that even the driest of experts can hardly ignore the Anti-Stratfordians. An objective account of what is really known about Shakespeare may, perhaps, dispel some fancies and fallacies.

Unprejudiced inquiry should begin with Shakespeare's works in their first state, to be found most conveniently in the Folio of 1623.

The first lines of the title page (see Pl. 2) read:

Mr. WILLIAM

SHAKESPEARES

COMEDIES,
HISTORIES, &
TRAGEDIES,

Publiſhed according to the True Originall Copies.

Beneath is the engraved portrait – not a masterpiece either of the engraver's or of the portrait painter's art, but at least recognizable. Everyone is familiar with that egg-shaped head and the bald dome.

The Folio is dedicated by its editors, John Heminges and Henry Condell

TO THE MOST NOBLE
AND
INCOMPARABLE PAIRE
OF BRETHREN
WILLIAM
Earle of Pembroke &c. Lord Chamberlaine to the
Kings Most Excellent Majestie

AND

PHILLIP
Earle of Montgomery, &c. Gentleman of his Maiesties
Bed-Chamber, Both Knights of the most Noble Order
of the Garter and our singular good
LORDS.

In the course of their dedicatory epistle, which is written in the obsequious and unctuous style common to such efforts, the editors tell us that these two noblemen had prosecuted both plays and author with much favour.

Then follows an address 'To the great Variety of Readers', exhorting them to buy the book, and giving the information that Shakespeare was a ready writer: 'His mind and hand went together; and what he thought, he vttered with that eaſineſſe, that wee haue ſcarſe receiued from him a blot in his papers.'

Next there is the memorial Ode by Ben Jonson in which Shakespeare is addressed as 'Sweet Swan of Avon'. Three lesser poets – Hugh Holland, L. Digges, and I. M. – add their tributes. Digges begins with the words:

> Shake-speare, at length thy pious fellowes giue
> The world thy Workes: thy Workes, by which, out-liue
> Thy Tombe, thy name muſt: when that stone is rent,
> And Time diſſolues thy Stratford Moniment,
> Here we aliue shall view thee still.

Then follows a list of 'The Names of the Principall Actors in

The Workes of William Shakespeare,

containing all his Comedies, Histories, and
Tragedies: Truely set forth, according to their first
ORIGINALL.

The Names of the Principall Actors
in all these Playes.

William Shakespeare.	Samuel Gilburne.
Richard Burbadge.	Robert Armin.
John Hemmings.	William Ostler.
Augustine Phillips.	Nathan Field.
William Kempt.	John Underwood.
Thomas Poope.	Nicholas Tooley.
George Bryan.	William Ecclestone.
Henry Condell.	Joseph Taylor.
William Slye.	Robert Benfield.
Richard Cowly.	Robert Goughe.
John Lowine.	Richard Robinson.
Samuell Crosse.	John Shancke.
Alexander Cooke.	John Rice.

3 The Actors' List from the First Folio, 1623

all these Plays' – twenty-six in all, headed by William Shakespeare, and including the names of Richard Burbage, John Heminges, Augustine Phillips, William Kempe, Henry Condell, Robert Armin, Nathan Field – all well-known actors of the time. (See Pl. 3.)

These preliminary pages of the Folio thus establish the fact that the author of the plays was Mr William Shakespeare of Stratford-on-Avon who was also a fellow actor of Heminges and Condell.* With such clear clues the biographer can begin his search for facts.

For the biography of an Elizabethan dramatist there are four sources of information, viz.: (*a*) his works; (*b*) the comments of contemporaries; (*c*) traditions and gossip; (*d*) documentary records.

(*a*) Shakespeare has left thirty-seven plays, the Sonnets, two long narrative poems, and a few minor short poems. The Sonnets – if they are autobiographical – tell a story of an intimate friendship with a young man of better social standing, of quarrels and reconciliations, of a rival poet, of a love affair with a faithless dark woman. Since, however, neither the young man nor the dark woman has as yet been certainly identified, the Sonnets cannot be regarded as 'biographical evidence'.

Nor are the plays, by themselves, reliable material for a biographer. Shakespeare has said so much that it is impossible to know when he himself is speaking out of his own experience or creating experiences proper to his characters, but it is, and must be, generally true that no writer who portrays a wide variety of characters and shows acquaintance with so wide a range of human

---

* Unless, of course, – as the Anti-Stratfordians maintain – the Folio was an elaborate fraud concocted by Heminges, Condell, Jonson, Digges, and by Isaac Jaggard and Edward Blount, who published the book, with the connivance of the two illustrious noblemen, and the actors listed in Pl. 3. If so, no one revealed the secret.

experience can have lived all his life in a narrow or confined environment. All great writers to some extent betray themselves. It is not difficult to guess that Jane Austen lived in a genteel circle or that the social background of Thackeray differed considerably from that of Dickens.

(*b*) There are many early references to Shakespeare, collected in *The Shakespeare Allusion Book* (2 vols., 1932), of which more than one hundred and fifty were made before Shakespeare's death. Most of them are mentions of plays or of characters or obvious borrowings of lines; they seldom give any facts about the man himself.

(*c*) Traditions are of varying value, and frequently can neither be tested nor trusted. There is only one contemporary anecdote about Shakespeare, recorded in 1602 in the diary of John Manningham, a barrister; it is possibly an invented jest.

Upon a time when Burbage played Richard III there was a Citizen grew so far in liking with him, that before she went from the play she appointed him to come that night unto her by the name of Richard the Third. Shakespeare, overhearing their conclusion, went before, was entertained, and at his game ere Burbage came. Then a message being brought that Richard the Third was at the door, Shakespeare caused return to be made that William the Conqueror was before Richard the Third.

John Aubrey,* a gentleman of the Restoration period, and a great collector of gossip, recorded a few anecdotes in his notebooks, including traditions which he gathered at second and third hand from an old actor called William Beeston, who was the son of one of Shakespeare's fellow actors. The most important of Aubrey's notes tell that Shakespeare was 'a handsome, well-shaped man : very good company, and of a very ready and pleasant smooth wit.' He heard also from Beeston that 'though, as Ben Jonson says of him, that he had but little Latin and less Greek,

* See *Aubrey's Brief Lives*, edited by Oliver Lawson Dick, 1949.

4 A bedroom in the Shakespeare House, Henley Street, Stratford-
on-Avon

he understood Latin pretty well: for he had been in his younger
years a schoolmaster in the country.'

Thomas Betterton, a famous actor of Restoration times, went
down to Stratford-on-Avon to examine the town records; and
there he collected from local inhabitants some stories which he
handed over to Nicholas Rowe, who used them in his introduction. As Rowe's note is the first serious account of Shakespeare
that survives, the biographical section is worth reproducing in
full:

It seems to be a kind of respect due to the memory of excellent men, especially of those whom their wit and learning have made famous, to deliver some account of themselves, as well as their works, to posterity. For this reason, how fond do we see some people of discovering any little personal story of the great men of antiquity! their families, the common incidents of their lives, and even their shape, make, and

5 Clopton Bridge, Stratford-on-Avon, built late in the fifteenth century

feature, have been the subject of critical inquiries. How trifling soever this curiosity may seem to be, it is certainly very natural; and we are hardly satisfied with an account of any remarkable person, till we have heard him described even to the very clothes he wears. As for what relates to men of letters, the knowledge of an author may sometimes conduce to the better understanding his book; and though the works of Mr Shakspere may seem to many not to want a comment, yet, I fancy, some little account of the man himself may not be thought improper to go along with them.

He was the son of Mr John Shakspere, and was born at Stratford-upon-Avon, in Warwickshire, in April 1564. His family, as appears by the register and publick writings relating to that town, were of good figure and fashion there, and are mentioned as gentlemen. His father, who was a considerable dealer in wool, had so large a family, ten children in all, that though he was his eldest son, he could give him no better education than his own employment. He had bred him, it is true, for some time at a free-school, where, it is probable, he acquired what Latin he was master of: but the narrowness of his circumstances, and the want of his assistance at home, forced his father to withdraw him from thence, and unhappily prevented his further proficiency in that language. It is, without controversy, that in his works we scarce find any traces of anything that looks like an imitation of the ancients. The delicacy of his taste, and the natural bent of his own great *genius* (equal, if not superior, to some of the best of theirs), would certainly have led him to read and study them with so much pleasure, that some of their fine images would naturally have insinuated themselves into, and been mixed with, his own writings; so that his not copying at least something from them, may be an argument of his never having read them. Whether his ignorance of the ancients were a disadvantage to him or no, may admit of a dispute: for though the knowledge of them might have made him more correct, yet it is not improbable but that the regularity and deference for them, which would have attended that correctness, might have restrained some of that fire, impetuosity, and even beautiful extravagance, which we admire in Shakespere: and I believe we are better pleased with those thoughts, altogether new and uncommon, which his own imagination supplied him so abundantly with, than if he had given us the most beautiful passages out of the Greek and Latin poets, and that in the most agreeable manner that it was possible for a master of the English language to deliver them.

Upon his leaving school, he seems to have given entirely into that way of living which his father proposed to him; and, in order to settle in the world after a family manner, he thought fit to marry while he was yet very young. His wife was the daughter of one Hathaway, said to have been a substantial yeoman in the neighbourhood of Stratford. In this kind of settlement he continued for some time, till an extravagance, that he was guilty of, forced him both out of his country, and that way of living, which he had taken up; and though it seemed at first to be a blemish upon his good manners, and a misfortune to him, yet it afterwards happily proved the occasion of exerting one of the greatest *geniuses* that ever was known in dramatick poetry. He had, by a misfortune common enough to young fellows, fallen into ill company; and, amongst them, some that made a frequent practice of deer-stealing,

6 Mason's Court, Rother Street, Stratford-on-Avon

engaged him more than once in robbing a park that belonged to Sir Thomas Lucy, of Cherlecot, near Stratford. For this he was prosecuted by that gentleman, as he thought, somewhat too severely: and, in order to revenge that ill usage, he made a ballad upon him. And though this, probably the first essay of his poetry, be lost, yet it is said to have been so very bitter, that it redoubled the prosecution against him to that

degree, that he was obliged to leave his business and family in Warwickshire for some time, and shelter himself in London.

It is at this time, and upon this accident, that he is said to have made
his first acquaintance in the playhouse.* He was received into the company then in being, at first in a very mean rank; but his admirable wit,
and the natural turn of it to the stage, soon distinguished him, if not as
an extraordinary actor, yet as an excellent writer. His name is printed,
as the custom was in those times, amongst those of the other players,
before some old plays, but without any particular account of what sort
of parts he used to play; and, though I have inquired, I could never meet
with any further account of him this way, than that the top of his performance was the Ghost in his own *Hamlet*. I should have been much
more pleased to have learned, from certain authority, which was the
first play he wrote; it would be, without doubt, a pleasure to any man,
curious in things of this kind, to see and know what was the first essay
of a fancy like Shakspere's. Perhaps we are not to look for his beginnings, like those of other authors, among their least perfect writings; art
had so little, and nature had so large a share in what he did, that for
aught I know, the performances of his youth, as they were the most
vigorous, and had the most fire and strength of imagination in them,
were the best. I would not be thought by this to mean, that this fancy
was so loose and extravagant, as to be independent on the rule and
government of judgement; but that what he thought was commonly so
great, so justly and rightly conceived in itself, that it wanted little or no
correction, and was immediately approved by an impartial judgement
at the first sight. But though the order of time in which the several
pieces were written be generally uncertain, yet there are passages in
some few of them which seem to fix their dates. So the *Chorus* at the end
of the fourth act of *Henry the Fifth*, by a compliment very handsomely
turned to the earl of Essex, shews the play to have been written when
that lord was general for the queen in Ireland; and his eulogy upon
queen Elizabeth, and her successor king James, in the latter-end of his

---

* There is a stage tradition, that his first office in the theatre was that of
prompter's attendant; whose employment it is to give the performers
notice to be ready to enter as often as the business of the play requires their
appearance on the stage.

Malone, *The Life of William Shakespeare*, 1821.

Henry the Eighth, is a proof of that play's being written after the accession of the latter of those two princes to the crown of England. Whatever the particular times of his writing were, the people of his age, who began to grow wonderfully fond of diversions of this kind, could not but be highly pleased, to see a *Genius* arise from amongst them of so pleasurable, so rich a vein, and so plentifully capable of furnishing their favourite entertainments. Besides the advantages of his wit, he was in himself a good-natured man, of great sweetness in his manners, and a most agreeable companion; so that it is no wonder, if, with so many good qualities, he made himself acquainted with the best conversations of those times. Queen Elizabeth had several of his plays acted before her, and without doubt gave him many gracious marks of her favour: it is that maiden princess plainly, whom he intends by

> . . . A fair vestal, throned by the west.
> *Midsummer Night's Dream.*

And that whole passage is a compliment very properly brought in, and very handsomely applied to her. She was so well pleased with that admirable character of Falstaff, in *The two Parts of Henry the Fourth*, that she commanded him to continue it for one play more, and to shew him in love. This is said to be the occasion of his writing *The Merry Wives of Windsor*. How well she was obeyed, the play itself is an admirable proof. Upon this occasion it may not be improper to observe, that this part of Falstaff is said to have been written originally under the name of *Oldcastle*; some of that family being then remaining, the queen was pleased to command him to alter it; upon which he made use of Falstaff. The present offence was indeed avoided; but I do not know whether the author may not have been somewhat to blame in his second choice, since it is certain that Sir John Falstaff, who was a knight of the garter, and a lieutenant-general, was a name of distinguished merit in the wars in France in Henry the Fifth's and Henry the Sixth's times. What grace soever the queen conferred upon him, it was not to her only he owed the fortune which the reputation of his wit made. He had the honour to meet with many great and uncommon marks of favour and friendship from the earl of Southampton, famous in the histories of that time for his friendship to the unfortunate earl of Essex. It was to that noble lord that he dedicated his poem of *Venus and Adonis*. There is one instance so singular in the magnificence of this patron of Shakspere's, that, if I had not been assured that the story was handed down by Sir William D'Avenant, who was probably very well acquainted with his affairs, I should not have ventured to have inserted, that my lord Southampton at one time gave him a thousand pounds, to enable him to go through with a purchase which he heard he had a mind to; a bounty very great, and very rare at any time, and almost equal to that profuse generosity the present age hath shewn to French dancers and Italian singers.

7 Part of the wall-painting in the White Swan Hotel, Stratford-on-Avon, showing a scene from the Book of Tobit, painted about 1560

What particular habitude or friendships he contracted with private men, I have not been able to learn, more than that every one, who had a true taste of merit, and could distinguish men, had generally a just value and esteem for him. His exceeding candour and good-nature must certainly have inclined all the gentler part of the world to love him, as the power of his wit obliged the men of the most delicate knowledge and polite learning to admire him.

His acquaintance with Ben Jonson began with a remarkable piece of humanity and good nature. Mr Jonson, who was at that time altogether unknown to the world, had offered one of his plays to the players, in order to have it acted; and the persons into whose hands it was put, after having turned it carelessly and superciliously over, were just upon returning it to him with an ill-natured answer, that it would be of no service to their company; when Shakspere luckily cast his eye upon it, and found something so well in it, as to engage him first to read it through, and afterwards to recommend Mr Jonson and his writings to the public. Jonson was certainly a very good scholar, and in that had the advantage of Shakspere; though at the same time, I believe, it must be allowed, that what Nature gave the latter was more than a balance for what books had given the former; and the judgement of a great man upon this occasion was, I think, very just and proper. In a conversation between Sir John Suckling, Sir William D'Avenant, Endymion Porter, Mr Hales of Eton, and Ben Jonson; Sir John Suckling, who was a professed admirer of Shakspere, had undertaken his defence against Ben Jonson with some warmth; Mr Hales, who had sat still for some time, told them, *That if Mr Shakspere had not read the ancients, he had likewise not stolen anything from them; and that if he would produce any one topick finely treated by any one of them, he would undertake to shew something upon the same subject, at least as well written, by Shakspere.*

The latter part of his life was spent, as all men of good sense will wish theirs may be, in ease, retirement, and the conversation of his friends. He had the good fortune to gather an estate equal to his occasion, and, in that, to his wish; and is said to have spent some years before his death at his native Stratford. His pleasurable wit and good-nature engaged

8 Harvard House, Stratford-on-Avon, home of Katherine Rogers, mother of John Harvard, the founder of Harvard College

him in the acquaintance, and entitled him to the friendship, of the gentlemen of the neighbourhood. Amongst them, it is a story almost still remembered in that country, that he had a particular intimacy with Mr Combe, an old gentleman noted thereabouts for his wealth and usury; it happened, that in a pleasant conversation amongst their common friends, Mr Combe told Shakspere, in a laughing manner, that he fancied he intended to write his epitaph, if he happened to out-live him; and since he could not know what might be said of him when he was dead, he desired it might be done immediately: upon which Shakspere gave him these four verses:

> Ten in the hundred lies here engrav'd,
> 'Tis a hundred to ten his soul is not sav'd:
> If any man ask, Who lies in this tomb?
> Oh! oh! quoth the devil, 'tis my John-a-Combe.

But the sharpness of the satire is said to have stung the man so severely, that he never forgave it.

He died in the 53rd year of his age, and was buried on the north side of the chancel, in the great church at Stratford, where a monument, as engraved in the plate, is placed in the wall. On his grave-stone underneath is,

> Good friend: for Jesus' sake forbear
> To dig the dust inclosed here.
> Blest be the man that spares these stones,
> And curst be he that moves my bones.*

He had three daughters, of which two lived to be married: Judith, the elder, to one Mr Thomas Quiney, by whom she had three sons, who all died without children; and Susanna, who was his favourite, to Dr John Hall, a physician of good reputation in that country. She left one child only, a daughter, who was married, first, to Thomas Nash, esq. and

---

* 'And curst be he that moves my bones.' See Pl. 18.

'It is uncertain whether this epitaph was written by Shakspere himself, or by one of his friends after his death. The imprecation contained in this last line, might have been suggested by an apprehension that our author's remains might share the same fate with those of the rest of his countrymen, and be added to the immense pile of human bones deposited in the charnel-house at Stratford. This, however, is mere conjecture; for similar execrations are found in many ancient Latin epitaphs.'

Malone.

afterwards to Sir John Bernard of Abbington, but died likewise without issue.

Other anecdotes were current in the eighteenth century. One of the more popular is that on his way to and from London, Shakespeare used to stay at the Crown Inn in Oxford kept by a melancholy innkeeper called John Davenant. Davenant's son William (1606–68), who became famous as a poet and dramatist of the Restoration, was Shakespeare's godson. It was a tradition in Oxford that the boy was

so fond of Shakespeare, that whenever he heard of his arrival, he would fly from school to see him. One day an old townsman observing the boy running homeward almost out of breath, asked him whither he was posting in that heat and hurry. He answered, to see his *god*-father Shakespeare. There's a good boy, said the other, but have a care that you don't take *God's* name in vain.

This version occurs in some notes left by William Oldys, an antiquarian who died in 1761.

Oldys also recorded that

One of Shakespeare's younger brothers, who lived to a good old age, even some years, as I compute, after the restoration of *K. Charles II*, would in his younger days come to London to visit his brother *Will*, as he called him, and be a spectator of him as an actor in some of his own plays. This custom, as his brother's fame enlarged, and his dramatic entertainments drew the greatest support of our principal, if not of all our theatres, he continued it seems so long after his brother's death, as even to the latter end of his own life. The curiosity at this time of the most noted actors to learn something from him of his brother, &c. they justly held him in the highest veneration. And it may well be believed, as there was besides a kinsman and descendant of the family, who was then a celebrated actor among them, this opportunity made them greedily inquisitive into every little circumstance, more especially in his dramatick character, which his brother could relate of him. But he, it seems, was so stricken in years, and possibly his memory so weakened with infirmities (which might make him the easier pass for a man of weak intellects) that he could give them but little light into their enquiries; and all that could be recollected from him of his brother *Will*, in that station was, the faint, general, and almost lost ideas he had of having once seen him act a part in one of his own comedies, wherein being to personate a decrepit old man, he wore a long beard, and appeared so weak and drooping and unable to walk, that he was forced to be supported and carried by another person to a table, at which he was seated among some company, who were eating, and one of them sang a song.

If this story is true, it seems that Shakespeare took the part of old Adam in *As You Like It*.

Another popular story, which originated from Rowe, is thus told by Dr Johnson:

In the time of *Elizabeth*, coaches being yet uncommon, and hired coaches not at all in use, those who were too proud, too tender, or too idle to walk, went on horseback to any distant business or diversion. Many came on horse-back to the play, and when *Shakespear* fled to *London* from the terrour of a criminal prosecution, his first expedient was to wait at the door of the play-house, and hold the horses of those that had no servants, that they might be ready again after the performance. In this office he became so conspicuous for his care and readiness, that in a short time every man as he alighted called for *Will. Shakespear*, and scarcely any other waiter was trusted with a horse while *Will. Shakespear* could be had. This was the first dawn of better fortune. *Shakespear* finding more horses put into his hand than he could hold, hired boys to wait under his inspection, who when *Will. Shakespear* was summoned, were immediately to present themselves, *I am* Shakespear's *boy*, *Sir*. In time *Shakespear* found higher employment, but as long as the practice of riding to the play-house continued, the waiters that held the horses retained the appellation of Shakespear's *Boys*.

The Rev. Richard Davies, a Gloucestershire parson and an antiquary who died in 1708, added to some notes on Shakespeare the observation that 'He died a papist.'*

* This, and all other records noted in this chapter, are included in E. K. Chambers' *William Shakespeare; A study of facts and problems*.

Such tales, though interesting, and sometimes possibly true, can seldom be verified. In an age of good conversation, a raconteur is more concerned with telling a good story than with its accuracy; and an anecdote always sounds more plausible when attached to some famous man.

(*d*) The fourth, and most important, sources for the biography of Shakespeare are official and documentary records, definite, reliable, and usually dull. Of prime importance is the register of Stratford-on-Avon which gives the date (and therefore fact) of the baptism of William Shakespeare and of his brothers and sisters and of his children, the date of burial of himself, and of his father, mother, and other relatives. His name is to be found in some records of lawsuits either as plaintiff, witness, or defendant. In the accounts of the Court of Queen Elizabeth and King James the sums paid to his Company are noted. His will survives in Somerset House.

The town records of Stratford-on-Avon show that Shakespeare's family was of good middle-class stock. Shakespeare was neither a 'peasant', nor a 'village lad', nor 'the Stratford clown'. Stratford-on-Avon in the sixteenth century was a small but important country town, and John Shakespeare, his father, was one of the wealthiest citizens who held in turn the chief municipal offices of the place. He had married, about 1557, Mary, the daughter of Robert Arden, who belonged to an ancient and distinguished Catholic family which suffered during the religious persecutions in Queen Elizabeth's reign. It is probable from recent researches that John Shakespeare himself was a zealous Catholic, and that William was brought up in the Old Faith. John and Mary Shakespeare had at least eight children, William being the third child and eldest son. He was baptized in the parish church of Stratford-on-Avon on 26 April 1564.

There are no records of his boyhood; it would be surprising if there were. A good education was available at the grammar

school, of which the masters were competent scholars from Oxford. Unfortunately the early school records have perished. Nor were the better-class inhabitants of Stratford either bookless or illiterate. Several of Shakespeare's younger contemporaries and friends of the family went up to Oxford University.

In the ecclesiastical records of Worcester there is a bond dated 27 November 1582, indemnifying the Bishop of Worcester in any action that might arise by means of any pre-contract, consanguinity, affinity, or by any other lawful means if William Shakespeare (his name is spelt Shagspere) and Ann Hathaway are married. The sureties were Fulke Sandall and John Richardson, friends of the bride. Shakespeare was aged 18½ and Ann, if the dates on her gravestone are correct, was aged 26. Nor was Ann Hathaway a peasant. Visitors to Stratford-on-Avon go to Shottery to see 'Ann Hathaway's Cottage', but the house is far from being a cottage (see Pl. 9). It is the dwelling of a yeoman of means, as can be seen from the carved four-poster bed, and the panelling. There is no need to sentimentalize the courtship. Five months later, on 26 May 1583, Susanna, their first child, was baptized, and on 22 February 1585, twins, Hamnet and Judith, were baptized. Apart from these records, no fact in Shakespeare's early biography is recorded in any official document.

It is not known when Shakespeare first appeared in London. The essential years, when most men collect their experiences, are missing. The various traditions have already been noted – that he was obliged to leave Stratford because he was in trouble for poaching deer from Sir Thomas Lucy, the great man of those parts; that for a time he was a schoolmaster in the country; that he first entered the theatre in some mean employment. But they do not account for everything.

It is not until 1592 that Shakespeare emerges as a person at the

9 The Hathaway House, Shottery, traditionally the home of Shakespeare's wife

TO THE RIGHT
HONOVRABLE, HENRY
VVriothesley, Earle of Southhampton,
and Baron of Titchfield.

THE loue I dedicate to your
Lordſhip is without end:wher-
of this Pamphlet without beginning is but a ſuperfluous
Moity. The warrant I haue of
your Honourable diſpoſition,
not the worth of my vntutord
Lines makes it aſſured of acceptance. VVhat I haue
done is yours, what I haue to doe is yours, being
part in all I haue, deuoted yours . VVere my worth
greater, my duety would ſhew greater, meane time,
as it is,it is bound to your Lordſhip; To whom I wiſh
long life ſtill lengthned with all happineſſe.

Your Lordſhips in all duety.

William Shakeſpeare.

A 2

centre of English life. He was then aged 28. Nor is this ignorance confined to Shakespeare. Very little is known of what was happening in the Elizabethan theatres before 1592, although at this time there were three London theatres and several London companies, who must between them have been producing at least fifty new plays a year. Yet of the plays written for the professional companies between 1560 and 1590 less than half a dozen have survived in print. Hitherto no one thought that such plays were worth printing, reading, or recording. Critics assume that in the public theatres plays were crude doggerel until Christopher Marlowe first showed his fellows how to write blank verse in *Tamburlaine*; they assume that Kyd's *Spanish Tragedy* and Greene's *Friar Bacon* were quite new kinds. It may well be so, but there is no evidence. Accounts of what happened in the Elizabethan theatre before 1592 are, in fact, guesswork; but from this date onwards detailed records begin, and the development of English drama, though there are many gaps, can be traced.

From 1592 to 1602 Henslowe's *Diary* (see p. 77) gives a fairly complete picture of theatrical conditions and of the output of the companies with which he was connected. Unfortunately the Lord Chamberlain's Company, in which Shakespeare became a sharer, did not act in Henslowe's theatres, nor indeed did it come into existence until 1594.

From 1592 onwards there are many records of Shakespeare's name, and since it is sometimes questioned whether there are any reliable facts about him some of the more important may be noted.

On 18 April 1593, Shakespeare's first poem, *Venus and Adonis*, was entered for publication in the Stationers' Register, and soon afterwards printed, with a dedication to Henry Wriothesley,* Earl of Southampton:

Right Honourable,
I know not how I shall offend in dedicating my unpolished lines to

---

* Pronounced 'Risley'.

your Lordship, nor how the world will censure me for choosing so strong a prop to support so weak a burthen: only, if your Honour seem but pleased, I account myself highly praised, and vow to take advantage of all idle hours, till I have honoured you with some graver labour. But if the first heir of my invention prove deformed, I shall be sorry it had so noble a godfather, and never after ear so barren a land, for fear it yield me still so bad a harvest. I leave it to your honourable survey, and your Honour to your heart's content, which I wish may always answer your own wish, and the world's hopeful expectation.

Your Honour's in all duty,

WILLIAM SHAKESPEARE

The poem was immediately popular, and during the next few years was reprinted nine times. It was much praised, and established Shakespeare's reputation as a poet.

There was very little playing throughout 1593, for a particularly bad outbreak of the plague occurred. The theatres were shut up and the players went on tour. On 9 May 1594, Shakespeare's second poem, *The Rape of Lucrece*, was entered. This also was dedicated to the Earl of Southampton, but in far warmer terms:

The love I dedicate to your Lordship is without end; whereof this pamphlet, without beginning, is but a superfluous moiety. The warrant I have of your honourable disposition, not the worth of my untutored lines, makes it assured of acceptance. What I have done is yours, what I have to do is yours, being part in all I have, devoted yours. Were my worth greater, my duty would show greater; meantime, as it is, it is bound to your Lordship, to whom I wish long life, still lengthened with happiness.

Your Lordship's in all duty,

WILLIAM SHAKESPEARE

In the summer of 1594, the playing companies, which had been badly disorganized by the plague, began to drift back to London.

11 Henry Wriothesley, third Earl of Southampton. Portrait by an unknown artist, *c*. 1601–3

For a few days Edward Alleyn, the great tragedian, ran a combined company made up of the Lord Chamberlain's and the Lord Admiral's players at a theatre in Newington Butts. During these few days Henslowe records that they played *Hamlet*,* *The Taming of the Shrew*, and *Titus Andronicus*. The arrangement did not last long, and two new companies were formed. Alleyn went to play at the Rose Theatre and formed a new Lord Admiral's Company. Later in the autumn some of his former associates, including Richard Burbage and William Kempe, went to the Theatre in Shoreditch and there established a new Lord Chamberlain's Company. To this Company Shakespeare now belonged, and henceforward his life is bound up with it and actual records accumulate.

During the Christmas holidays of 1594–5, the Company acted twice at Court. There is an entry in the Chamber Accounts:

To William Kempe, William Shakespeare, and Richard Burbage, servants to the Lord Chamberlain, upon the Council's warrant dated at Whitehall 15 March 1594[–5] for two several comedies or interludes showed by them before her Majesty in Christmas time last past, viz. upon St Stephen's day and Innocent's day, £13 6s. 8d., and by way of her Majesty's reward £6 13s. 4d.

The Company acted regularly at Court at Christmas time, but as the later payments were made to John Heminges on their behalf, Shakespeare's name is not again mentioned in the accounts.

On 11 August 1596, the burial of Hamnet, son of William Shakespeare, is recorded in the Stratford Parish register.

On 20 October 1596, William Dethick, Garter Principal King of Arms, issued a grant of coat of arms to John Shakespeare of Stratford-on-Avon,

whose parents and late grandfather for his faithful and valiant service was advanced and rewarded by the most prudent prince, King Henry the Seventh, of famous memory, sithence which time they have con-

---

* Not the play as now known but an earlier version.

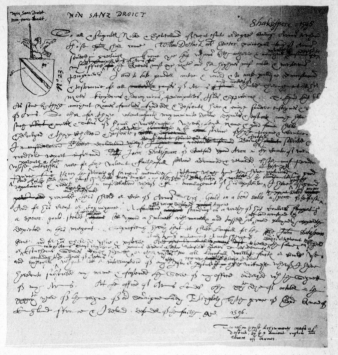

12 The first draft of Sir William Dethick's entries in the Heralds' College assigning arms to John Shakespeare, 1596–9

tinued at those parts being of good reputation and credit; and that the said John hath married the daughter and one of the heirs of Robert Arden of Wilmcote, in the said county, esquire; and for the encouragement of his posterity, to whom these achievements by the ancient custom of the Laws of Arms, may descend; I the said Garter King of Arms have assigned, granted, and by these presents confirmed: This shield or coat of arms, viz.: Gold, on a bend sable, a spear of the first, steeled argent. And for his crest or cognizance, a falcon, his wings displayed, argent, standing on a wreath of his colours; supporting a spear

gold steeled as aforesaid, set upon a helmet with mantels and tassels as hath been accustomed and doth more plainly appear depicted on this margin. Signifying hereby and by the authority of my office aforesaid ratifying that it shall be lawful for the said John Shakespeare gentleman and for his children, issue and posterity (at all times and places convenient) to bear and make demonstration of the same blazon or achievement upon their shields, targets, escutcheons, coats of arms, pennons, guidons, seals, rings, edifices, buildings, utensils, liveries, tombs or monuments, or otherwise for all lawful warlike facts of civil use and exercises, according to the Laws of Arms and customs that to Gentlemen belongeth, without let or interruption of any other person or persons for use or bearing the same.

The motto chosen was *Non sanz droict* – not without right: what significance lies behind this self-conscious challenge is not known. William Shakespeare was thus entitled to call himself 'gentleman'. (See Pl. 12.) The coat of arms is emblazoned on his monument in Stratford-on-Avon Church.

There was trouble for Shakespeare in this year, 1596, though the details are regrettably brief. In 1931 Leslie Hotson published his discovery* of a new reference to Shakespeare: a record that on 29 November William Wayt claimed sureties of the peace against William Shakespeare, Francis Langley (owner of the Swan Theatre), Dorothy Soer, and Ann Lee, for fear of death, and so forth. Unfortunately nothing is definitely known of the cause of William Wayt's anxieties.

On 4 May 1597, Shakespeare agreed to purchase from William Underhill, New Place, a large house in the centre of Stratford-on-Avon. The property included 'one messuage, two barns, and two gardens with the appurtenances', in return for which '*idem Willielmus Shakespeare dedit predicto Willielmo Underhill sexaginta libras sterlingorum*' – 'the same William Shakespeare gave

* In *Shakespeare versus Shallow*, 1931.

---

13 The garden and site of New Place, Stratford-on-Avon

14 The Town Hall and Chapel Street, Stratford-on-Avon, looking towards the site of New Place and the Guild Chapel

the said William Underhill sixty pounds sterling'. The house has long since been demolished, but as the foundations revealed, it was large, having a frontage of about sixty feet and a depth of about seventy.

On 29 August 1597, Andrew Wise entered for printing *The Tragedy of Richard the Second*, which was published soon after with the title page, 'The Tragedy of King Richard the Second. As it hath been publicly acted by the right Honourable the Lord Chamberlain his servants.' When a second and third edition appeared in 1598, Wise added 'By William Shake-speare'.

On 15 November 1597, the collectors of the subsidy for the ward of Bishopsgate, London, submitted a list of various persons from whom they could not collect their dues. Amongst those of St Helen's Parish was William Shakespeare, who owed 5s. Shakespeare's name appears in similar lists in 1598, 1599, and 1600.

In 1598 there was a considerable shortage of corn and a survey was taken of various holdings. In Stratford, William Shakespeare's name appears in the list taken on 4 February as holding ten quarters.

On 25 February 1598, Andrew Wise entered *The First Part of Henry the Fourth*, which appeared with the title 'The History of Henry the Fourth: With the battle at Shrewsbury, between the King and Lord Henry Percy, surnamed Henry Hotspur of the North. With the humorous conceits of Sir John Falstaff.'

On 22 July 1598, the Stationers' Register records that James Roberts entered 'for his copy under the hands of both the wardens, a book of the Merchant of Venice, or otherwise called the Jew of Venice, provided that it be not printed by the said James Roberts or any other whatsoever without licence first had from the Right honourable the Lord Chamberlain'. The book was afterwards transferred to Thomas Hayes, another printer, on 28 October 1600, who issued a Quarto with the title, 'The most excellent History of the Merchant of Venice. With the extreme cruelty of Shylock the Jew towards the said Merchant, in cutting a just pound of his flesh: and the obtaining of Portia by the choice of three chests. As it hath been divers time acted by the Lord Chamberlain his servants. Written by William Shakespeare.'

On 7 September 1598, Francis Meres' *Palladis Tamia*, with its praise of Shakespeare's work (see p. 13), was entered for publication.

In September 1598, Ben Jonson's *Every Man in His Humour* was acted by the Lord Chamberlain's men. In the Folio edition of Jonson's plays, published in 1616, he noted:

This comedy was first acted, in the year 1598. By the then L. Chamberlain his servants. The Principal comedians were:

Will. Shakespeare.	Ric. Burbage
Aug. Philips.	Joh. Hemings
Hen. Condel.	Tho. Pope.
Will. Slye.	Chr. Beeston.
Will. Kempe.	Joh. Duke.

On October 1598, Richard Quiney, a Stratford friend, was in London, and wrote to Shakespeare the following letter:

Loving Countryman, I am bold of you as of a friend, craving your help with thirty pounds upon Mr Bushell's and my security or Mr Mytton's with me. Mr Rosswell is not come to London as yet, and I have especial cause. You shall friend me much in helping me out of all the debts I owe in London, I thank God, and much quiet my mind which would not be indebted. I am now towards the Court, in hope of answer for the despatch of my business. You shall neither lose credit nor money by me, the Lord willing, and now but persuade yourself so as I hope, and you shall not need to fear, but with all hearty thankfulness I will hold my time, and content your friend, and if we bargain farther you shall be the paymaster yourself. My time bids me hasten to an end, and so I commit this to your care and hope of your help. I fear I shall not be back this night from the Court. Haste. The Lord be with you and with us all, Amen. From the Bell in Carter Lane, the 25 October 1598. Yours in all kindness. Ryc. Quyney.

The letter, now in the Birthplace Museum at Stratford, was addressed 'To my loving good friend and my countryman Mr Wm Shakespeare deliver these.'

Some time in 1598 Cuthbert Burby printed 'A Pleasant Conceited Comedy called, Love's Labour's Lost. As it was presented before her Highness this last Christmas. Newly corrected and augmented by W. Shakespere.'

In 1599 a dainty little octavo was printed with the title 'The Passionate Pilgrim By W. Shakespeare' – a made-up volume, containing some sonnets from Shakespeare's plays, some sonnets which afterwards appeared in the volume of Sonnets, and a number of poems by other men.

On 23 August 1600, Andrew Wise and William Aspley entered in the Stationers' Register 'the second part of the History of King Henry the iiijth with the humours of Sir John Falstaff: written by Master Shakespeare'. The Quarto appeared with the title 'The Second Part of Henry the Fourth, continuing to his death, and coronation of Henry the Fifth. With the humours of Sir John Falstaff, and swaggering Pistol. As it hath been sundry times publicly acted by the right honourable, the Lord Chamberlain his servants. Written by William Shakespeare.'

On the same day Andrew Wise and William Aspley also entered *Much Ado about Nothing* 'written by Master Shakespeare'. Again the title page reads 'As it hath been sundry times publicly acted by the right honourable the Lord Chamberlain his servants. Written by William Shakespeare.'

On 8 October 1600, Thomas Fisher entered *A Midsummer Night's Dream* which was published 'As it hath been sundry times publicly acted, by the right honourable, the Lord Chamberlain his servants. Written by William Shakespeare.'

On 8 September 1601, the burial of Mr John Shakespeare, Shakespeare's father, is recorded in the Stratford Parish register.

On 18 January 1602, *The Merry Wives of Windsor* was entered by John Busby. The text which he printed was pirated* and hopelessly corrupt, but the title page gives some interesting information. 'A most pleasant and excellent conceited Comedy, of Sir John Falstaff, and the Merry Wives of Windsor. Entermixed with sundry variable and pleasing humours of Sir Hugh the Welsh Knight, Justice Shallow, and his wise cousin M. Slender. With the swaggering vein of Auncient Pistol, and Corporal Nym. By William Shakespeare. As it hath been divers times acted by the

---

* Pirated – i.e. a corrupt text, based on a copy not authorized by the original writer or owner.

A
Most pleasaunt and
excellent conceited Co-
medie, of Syr *Iohn Falstaffe*, and the
merrie Wiues of *Windsor*.

Entermixed with sundrie
variable and pleasing humors, of Syr *Hugh*
the Welch Knight, Iustice *Shallow*, and his
wife Cousin M. *Slender*.

With the swaggering vaine of Auncient
Pistoll, and Corporall *Nym*.

By *William Shakespeare*.

As it hath bene diuers times Acted by the right Honorable
my Lord Chamberlaines seruants. Both before her
Maiestie, and else-where.

LONDON
Printed by T. C. for Arthur Iohnson, and are to be sold at
his shop in Powles Church-yard, at the signe of the
Flower de Leuse and the Crowne.
1602.

right Honourable my Lord Chamberlain's servants. Both before her Majesty, and elsewhere.'

On 1 May 1602, an agreement was made between William Combe of Warwick, Esquire, and John Combe of Stratford on the one part, and William Shakespeare of Stratford-on-Avon, Gentleman of the other part, whereby the Combes 'in consideration of the sum of three hundred and twenty pound of current English money' sold to Shakespeare one hundred and seven acres of arable land in the parish of Old Stratford.

On 28 September 1602, Shakespeare acquired a cottage in Chapel Lane, Stratford-on-Avon. The transfer is recorded in the Court Roll of Rowington Manor: '*unum cotagium cum pertinenciis scitiatum iacens et existens in Stratford super Avon, in quodam vico ibidem vocato Walkers Street alias Dead Lane, ad opus et usum Willielmi Shackespere*'.

On 19 May 1603 letters patent were issued appointing the former Lord Chamberlain's Company to be the King's Players. The patent records:

James by the grace of God, etc. To all Justices, Mayors, Sheriffs, Constables, Headboroughs, and other our officers and loving subjects, greeting. Know ye that We of our special grace, certain knowledge, and mere motion, have licensed and authorized and by these presents do license and authorize these our servants Lawrence Fletcher, William Shakespeare, Richard Burbage, Augustine Phillips, John Hemings, Henry Condell, William Sly, Robert Armin, Richard Cowley and the rest of their associates, freely to use and exercise the art and faculty of playing Comedies, Tragedies, Histories, Interludes, Morals, Pastorals, stage plays, and such others, like as they have already studied or hereafter shall use or study, as well for the recreation of our loving subjects as for our solace and pleasure when we shall think good to see them during our pleasure.

In 1603 Ben Jonson's *Sejanus* was acted. The folio edition of 1616 notes 'This Tragedy was first acted, in the year 1603. By the

15 Title-page of the 'Bad' Quarto of *The Merry Wives of Windsor*, 1602

THE
Tragicall Historie of
HAMLET,

Prince of Denmarke.

By William Shakespeare.

Newly imprinted and enlarged to almost as much
againe as it was, according to the true and perfect
Coppie.

AT LONDON,
Printed by I. R. for N. L. and are to be sold at his
shoppe vnder Saint Dunstons Church in
Fleetstreet. 1605.

King's Majesty's servants. The principal tragedians were,

Ric. Burbage.	Will. Shakespeare.
Aug. Phillips.	Joh. Hemings.
Will. Sly.	Hen. Condell.
Joh. Lowin.	Alex. Cooke.'

Some time in 1603 a pirated, and very bad text of *Hamlet* was printed entitled 'The Tragical History of Hamlet Prince of Denmark. By William Shake-speare. As it hath been divers times acted by his Highness' servants in the City of London: as also in the two Universities of Cambridge and Oxford, and elsewhere.' Another edition, the fullest of the early texts of *Hamlet* that exists, came out in 1604 with the title 'The Tragical History of Hamlet, Prince of Denmark. By William Shakespeare. Newly imprinted and enlarged to almost as much again as it was, according to the true and perfect copy.'

In March 1604, King James made a 'royal proceeding' through the City of London. The players as servants of the Chamber were given red cloth for their liveries. The list of recipients each of four yards was: William Shakespeare, Augustine Phillips, Lawrence Fletcher, John Heminges, Richard Burbage, William Sly, Robert Armin, Henry Condell, Richard Cowley.

On 4 May 1605, Augustine Phillips was dying and made his will. He left bequests of gold pieces to his fellow actors. Shakespeare was mentioned first. 'I give and bequeath to my fellow, William Shakespeare, a thirty-shilling piece in gold.' To Condell he also left a thirty-shilling piece; to five other members of the Company a twenty-shilling piece.

On 24 July 1605, Ralph Huband of Ippesley 'for and in consideration of the sum of four hundred and forty pounds of lawful English money' assigned to William Shakespeare one half of all the tithes of Stratford, Old Stratford, Welcombe, and Bishopton, and half the tithes of the parish of Stratford-on-Avon. The annual value was £60.

16 Title-page of the 'Good' Quarto of *Hamlet*, 1604–5

On 5 June 1607, the marriage of John Hall, Gentleman, and Susanna Shakespeare (Shakespeare's elder daughter) is recorded in the Stratford Parish register.

On 26 November 1607 was entered 'Master William Shakespeare his history of King Lear, as it was played before the King's Majesty at Whitehall upon Saint Stephen's night at Christmas last, [i.e. 26 December 1606] by his Majesty's servants playing usually at the Globe on the Bankside.' This information was repeated on the title page.

On 9 September 1608, the burial of Mary Shakespeare, widow (Shakespeare's mother), is recorded in the Stratford Parish register.

On 11 May 1612, Shakespeare was an important witness in a domestic lawsuit in which it was shown that about 1604 he was boarding in the house of Christopher Mountjoy, a Huguenot tire-maker*, near St Olave's Church, Cripplegate. Mountjoy's daughter married his apprentice named Stephen Bellott. Shakespeare had helped to make the match. In 1612 Bellott was suing his father-in-law for failing to give his daughter the portion agreed. Shakespeare was a principal witness and his testimony is headed 'William Shakespeare of Stratford upon Avon, in the County of Warwick, gentleman, of the age of forty-eight years or thereabouts, sworn and examined the day and year above said, deposeth and saith'. The answers to the five interrogatories were then recorded and he signed the document at the foot.

On 31 March 1613, the Steward of the Earl of Rutland paid to 'Mr Shakespeare in gold about My Lord's *impressa* 44s.; to Richard Burbage for painting and making it, in gold 44s.' The *impressa* was a shield painted with a symbolical device and mottoes borne at the tilting on the King's accession day.

On 28 January 1613, John Combe, a wealthy Stratford land-owner, made his will, which included the bequest to 'Mr William Shakespeare five pounds'.

On 10 March 1613, Henry Walker, citizen and minstrel of

* A tire was a woman's head-dress.

London, assigned a dwelling place or tenement in the precinct of Blackfriars, 'part of which said tenement is erected over a great gate leading to a capital messuage', to William Shakespeare of Stratford-on-Avon, in the County of Warwick, Gentleman, William Johnson, citizen and vintner of London (and host of the Mermaid Tavern), John Jackson, and John Heminges of London, Gentlemen, for one hundred and forty pounds.

On 10 February 1616, the marriage of Thomas Quyny and Judith Shakespeare (Shakespeare's younger daughter) is recorded in the Stratford Parish register.

On 25 March 1616, Shakespeare executed his will, a lengthy document (now in Somerset House) on three sheets of parchment, each of which he signed. As it gives a clear picture of his family relationship, it is worth reprinting in full:

In the name of God, Amen. I William Shakespeare, of Stratford upon Avon in the county of Warr., gent., in perfect health and memory, God be praised, do make and ordain this my last will and testament in manner and form following. That is to say, First, I commend my soul into the hands of God my Creator, hoping and assuredly believing, through the only merits of Jesus Christ my Saviour, to be made partaker of life everlasting, and my body to the earth whereof it is made.

Item, I give and bequeath unto my daughter Judith one hundred and fifty pounds of lawful English money, to be paid unto her in the manner and form following; that is to say, one hundred pounds in discharge of her marriage portion within one year after my decease, with consideration after the rate of two shillings in the pound for so long time as the same shall be unpaid unto her after my decease, and the fifty pounds residue thereof upon her surrendering of or giving of such sufficient security as the overseers of this my will shall like of, to surrender or grant, all her estate and right that shall descend or come unto her after my decease, or that she now hath, of, in, or to, one copy-hold tenement, with the appurtenances, lying and being in Stratford upon Avon aforesaid in the said county of Warr., being parcel or holden of the manor of Rowington, unto my daughter Susanna Hall and her heirs forever.

Item, I give and bequeath unto my said daughter Judith one hundred and fifty pounds more, if she or any issue of her body be living at the end of three years next ensuing the day of the date of this my will, during which time my executors to pay her consideration from my decease according to the rate aforesaid. And if she die within the said term without issue of her body, then my will is, and I do give and bequeath one hundred pounds thereof to my niece Elizabeth Hall, and the fifty pounds to be set forth by my executors during the life of my sister Joan Hart, and the use and profit thereof coming shall be paid to my said sister Joan, and after her decease the said £50 shall remain amongst the children of my said sister, equally to be divided amongst them. But if my said daughter Judith be living at the end of the said three years, or any issue of her body, then my will is, and so I devise and bequeath the said hundred and fifty pounds to be set out by my executors and over-seers for the best benefit of her and her issue, and the stock not to be paid unto her so long as she shall be married and covert baron; but my will is, that she shall have the consideration yearly paid unto her during her life, and, after her decease, the said stock and consideration to be paid to her children, if she have any, and if not to her executors or assigns, she living the said term after my decease. Provided that if such husband as she shall at the end of the said three years be married unto, or attain after, do sufficiently assure unto her and the issue of her body lands answerable to the portion of this my will given unto her, and to be adjudged so by my executors and overseers, then my will is, that the said £150 shall be paid to such husband as shall make assurance, to his own use.

Item, I give and bequeath unto my said sister Joan £20 and all my wearing apparel, to be paid and delivered within one year after my decease; And I do will and devise unto her the house with the appurten-ances in Stratford wherein she dwelleth, for her natural life, under the yearly rent of 12d.

Item, I give and bequeath unto her three sons, William Hart, — Hart, and Michael Hart, five pounds apiece, to be paid within one year after my decease.

Item, I give and bequeath unto the said Elizabeth Hall all my plate (except my broad silver and gilt bowl) that I now have at the date of this will.

Item, I give and bequeath unto the poor of Stratford aforesaid ten pounds; to Mr Thomas Combe my sword; to Thomas Russel, esquire, five pounds; and to Francis Collins, of the borough of Warr., in the county of Warr., gent., thirteen pounds, six shillings, and eight pence, to be paid within one year after my decease.

Item, I give and bequeath to Hamlet Sadler xxvis. viiid. to buy him a ring; to William Reynolds, gent., xxvis. viiid. to buy him a ring; to my godson William Walker xxs. in gold; to Anthony Nash, gent., xxvis. viiid.; and the Mr John Nash xxvis. viiid.; and to my fellows John Heminge, Richard Burbage, and Henry Condell, xxvis. viiid. apiece to buy them rings.

Item, I give, will, bequeath, and devise unto my daughter Susanna Hall, for better enabling of her to perform this my will, and towards the performance thereof, all that capital messuage or tenement with the appurtenances, in Stratford aforesaid, called the New Place wherein I now dwell, and two messuages or tenements with the appurtenances, situate, lying and being in Henley Street, within the borough of Stratford aforesaid; and all my barns, stables, orchards, gardens, lands, tenements, and hereditaments whatsoever, situate, lying and being or to be had, received, perceived, or taken, within the towns, hamlets, villages, fields, and grounds of Stratford upon Avon, Old Stratford, Bishopton, and Welcombe, or in any of them in the said county of Warr. And also all that messuage or tenement, with the appurtenances, wherein one John Robinson dwelleth, situate, lying, and being in the Blackfriars in London, near the Wardrobe; and all my other lands, tenements and hereditaments whatsoever, to have and to hold all and singular the said premises, with their appurtenances, unto the said Susanna Hall, for and during the term of her natural life, and after her decease, to the first son of her body lawfully issuing; and to the heirs males of the body of the first son lawfully issuing; and for default of such issue, to the second son of her body lawfully issuing, and to the heirs males of the body of the second son lawfully issuing; and for default of such heirs, to the third son of the body of the said Susanna lawfully issuing, and of the heirs males of the body of the said third son lawfully issuing; and for default of such issue, the same so to be and remain to the fourth, fifth, sixth, and seventh sons of her body issuing one after another and the heirs males of the bodies of the said fourth, fifth, sixth and seventh sons lawfully issuing, in such manner as it is

GOOD FREND FOR IESVS SAKE FORBEARE,
TO DIGG THE DVST ENCLOASED HEARE.
BLESE BE Y MAN Y SPARES HES STONES,
AND CVRST BE HE Y MOVES MY BONES.

18 Shakespeare's gravestone

before limited to be and remain to the first, second and third sons of her body, and to their heirs males; and for default of such issue, the said premises to be and remain to my said niece Hall, and the heirs males of her body lawfully issuing; and for default of such issue, to my daughter Judith, and the heirs males of her body lawfully issuing; and for default of such issue, to the right heirs of me the said William Shakespeare for ever.

Item, I give unto my wife my second best bed with the furniture. Item, I give and bequeath to my said daughter Judith my broad silver gilt bowl. All the rest of my goods, chattels, leases, plate, jewels, and

17 Shakespeare's monument in Holy Trinity Church, Stratford-on-Avon

household stuff whatsoever, after my debts and legacies paid, and my funeral expenses discharged, I give, devise and bequeath to my son-in-law, John Hall, gent., and my daughter Susanna his wife, whom I ordain and make executors of this my last will and testament.

And I do entreat and appoint the said Thomas Russell, esquire, and Francis Collins, gent., to be overseers hereof, and do revoke all former wills, and publish this to be my last will and testament. In witness thereof I have hereunto put my hand, the day and year first above written.

By me William Shakespeare.

On 23 April 1616, according to the inscription on the memorial in Stratford church, Shakespeare died, and on 25 April the burial of Will. Shakespeare, Gentleman, is recorded in the Stratford Parish register.

These are but a selection of actual records of various kinds which mention Shakespeare by name. They show that William Shakespeare of Stratford-on-Avon, after a youth and early manhood spent no one knows where, became a successful dramatist some time before the autumn of 1592; that in the autumn of 1594 he was a member of the Lord Chamberlain's Company which became the King's Company in 1603; that he wrote plays for his Company which were popular; that he prospered and made money which he invested in property at Stratford; and that he died and was buried in his native town. From these beginnings it is not impossible to build up a fairly full biography, for the life of the dramatist was bound up with the Company to which he belonged and for which he wrote his plays.

Nevertheless, though many of the main facts of Shakespeare's life and career are clearly and indisputably established, the intimate details which might have been recorded in letters, anecdotes, and sayings are lost. We can only know Shakespeare from the outside. Perhaps it is better so. Few great works of art are made more admirable by a candid biography of the author.

19 The nave of Holy Trinity Church, Stratford-on-Avon

3

The Scholarly Approach to Shakespeare

Some preliminary preparation is needed to understand any great works of art, and especially those which belong to a past age. Shakespeare was regarded as a great writer almost from the first, and the history of Shakespearean criticism mirrors the fluctuation in taste of the last 350 years. Since the beginning of the twentieth century there have been several new developments and changes of interest of all kinds.

In the year 1904 appeared a series of lectures originally delivered in the University of Oxford which caused considerable stir at the time; the volume was called *Shakespearean Tragedy*, and it was written by A. C. Bradley. The book was the culmination and the best example of over a century of Shakespearean criticism, which began with Maurice Morgann's *Essay on the dramatic character of Sir John Falstaff* (1777), and continued with Lamb and Coleridge, and throughout the nineteenth century. Bradley's attitude, in general, was that the characters in Shakespeare's plays were real men and women whose emotions, personalities, motives, and even past history, could be minutely examined, dissected, and discussed. Bradley wrote before the present enthusiasm for Freudian psychology, but his lectures were in the main psychological. In their own way they were magnificent, and the general feeling at the time amongst critics and readers was almost one of despair that the last words had been said, on the greater tragedies at least, and that nothing more remained to be done. Nevertheless, in the same year, 1904, appeared the first volumes of two works which considerably altered notions about Shakespeare and his plays: an edition of the works of the Elizabethan pamphleteer, Thomas Nashe, edited by R.B.McKerrow, and the *Diary* and *Papers* of Phillip Henslowe, edited by W.W.Greg. Both were fine pieces of scholarship.

McKerrow examined the different texts minutely, and by exact comparison and deduction he was able to reveal much that went on in the Elizabethan printing-houses, while by his illuminating commentary he illustrated contemporary thought and history. This work was one of the first great examples of the modern study of bibliography which showed scholars what could be recovered by exact examination of texts and manuscripts, and all that went to the making of a printed book.

The *Diary* and *Papers* of Phillip Henslowe were important in another way. Henslowe was the owner of several London theatres: the Rose, the Fortune, and others. For a period of ten years, between 1592 and 1602, he kept an exact account in a large ledger of his dealings with the various companies that played at his theatres. This account book, known as *Henslowe's Diary*, is the most valuable of all records of Elizabethan stage history.

In 1592 Edward Alleyn, the first Elizabethan tragic actor to become famous, married Henslowe's stepdaughter Joan Woodward, and for the next twenty-four years Henslowe and Alleyn worked closely together in partnership. After Henslowe's death in 1616 his papers passed to Alleyn. By this time Alleyn was a wealthy man, and in his old age he founded the College of God's Gift at Dulwich. When he died he bequeathed his collection of pictures to his foundation, and by surprising luck the papers have survived. As well as the *Diary*, they include contracts with actors, letters from dramatists, the agreement with the builder for building the Fortune Theatre, and many other documents which are invaluable.

Henslowe's *Diary* was first edited and published in 1845 by

John Payne Collier, a fine Elizabethan scholar. Unfortunately for some reason Collier, finding that his discoveries did not keep pace with his enthusiasms, began to invent Elizabethan documents and to forge additions in genuine manuscripts. When his forgeries were revealed, his work was naturally discredited and his edition of the *Diary* was so suspected that little attention was paid to it. Greg was easily able to clear the *Diary* of Collier's additions, and to show its importance for an understanding of the conditions of the Elizabethan stage. His edition of the *Diary* and *Papers* came out between 1904 and 1907.

Thereafter for some years the scholars had the field to themselves; it was quickly realized that once the conditions under which Shakespeare wrote were known, much light would be thrown on the making of his plays, and on their meaning. For a time the philosopher – for Bradley was philosopher rather than scholar – gave way to the antiquarian.

Today students of Shakespeare are interested mainly in two kinds of study which radiate from the plays. An intensive study of any one kind or all may bring us nearer understanding – or farther away – as they are used and followed. These kinds may be labelled Scholarly and Critical.

The scholar says in effect, 'Shakespeare's plays are now more than three hundred and fifty years old; since then the English language, manners, and ideas have changed greatly. To understand him therefore we must know Shakespeare's environment and examine his plays in the conditions of their original composition.'

The attitude of the critic, on the other hand, is that great literature is timeless and therefore perpetually modern. He is not concerned with antiquity but with certain works of dramatic art and how they concern him.

Modern scholars, in studying Shakespeare's plays, are concerned with a wide variety of interests, which may be subdivided into three main branches of study.

(*a*) The first consideration is to re-create the historical environment in which Shakespeare's plays were written. A working dramatist is concerned with entertaining his audience, and all acted drama directly or indirectly reflects the interests, taste, and ideas of the time of its first production. The events great and small that were happening around Shakespeare are therefore directly or indirectly part of his material. The scholar must know something of current notions and topics, of wars, excitements, depressions, panics, revolutions, scandals and gossip, of passing feelings and literary fashions, for fashions in literature changed even more quickly in Shakespeare's time than today. He must be familiar with ideas then current of literary criticism, science, psychology, history, morals, religion, theological controversy, astrology. All these affected Shakespeare immediately; they passed through the filter of his personality and were largely the material of his drama; for he, no less than other dramatists, supplied his audience with thoughts that were immediately interesting and exciting.

(*b*) As important for the understanding of drama is a study of the conditions of dramatic production; the details of the construction, arrangement, and conventions of the Elizabethan stage; the organization, finances, and history of the dramatic companies; the actors themselves, their styles and personalities; the audience and theatre-going public, its tastes and prejudices. These and other kindred matters affect the writing and acting of a play. All are relevant even to a most elementary understanding of Shakespeare's plays; had he written for a modern stage, the form and manner of his plays would have been quite different.

(*c*) Shakespeare's plays survive as printed texts. The conditions of publication are therefore important. The scholar must first study the history of a play's script, and how Elizabethan plays were in fact written. He must examine the earliest texts to see whether there are traces of revision or collaboration. He must know something of the methods of a printing-house, the habits of the reading public, the ways of the censor and how he worked.

He must study the history of each play from the time when the author first wrote it until, having passed through stage performance, it appeared as a printed Quarto; what happened between the printing of the Quarto* of an individual play and the time when it was printed with the rest of the plays in the Folio* of 1623; the changes that have occurred between the first printing of the Folio and the modern text. All these factors will affect the printed text which the reader of today uses, and which also gives the actor his lines for a performance on the stage.

Moreover words are constantly changing their meanings. It is obvious, for instance, at first reading that many of Shakespeare's words conveyed an essentially different meaning from modern usage. Since Shakespeare's birth, and especially in the first century thereafter, not only have new words been adapted into English, but words used by Shakespeare have changed their meanings and connotations. A first reading of *Lear* produces many words which send the reader to the dictionary or the footnotes for enlightenment, such as *character* (handwriting), *engine* (lever), *subscription* (allegiance, or a name written at the foot of a document), *addition* (a title added to a man's name, so honour), *latched* (lanced, wounded), *tax* (censure), *favour* (face), *fancy* (love). Sometimes all the words are familiar but the sense seems quite alien. When we are told of Lear that he has been 'confined to exhibition', it does not mean 'put in a cage like a monkey' but 'limited to an allowance of pocket money'. Or again, 'equalities are so weigh'd, that curiosity in neither can make choice of either's moiety' – what does it mean?

Far more difficult, and often quite beyond recall, are the subtler differences, the associations and ideas that cluster round the commonest of words, such as 'king' or 'prince', 'father', 'daughter', 'wife'. Whatever nowadays may be the normal associations of the word 'king', they are hardly those expressed (probably by Shakespeare himself) in the play of Sir Thomas More:

---

* For Quarto and Folio see pp. 206–7.

> For to the King God hath His office lent
> Of dread, of justice, power and command,
> Hath bid him rule, and will'd you to obey;
> And, to add ampler majesty to this,
> He hath not only lent the King his figure,
> His throne and sword, but given him his own Name,
> Calls him a god on earth. What do you then
> Rising 'gainst him that God Himself installs
> But rise 'gainst God?*

In this conception of the monarchy there is little room for a salaried official called the Leader of Her Majesty's Opposition.

Nor again, even in old-fashioned families, does a modern father arrange a marriage for his daughter without consulting her, as Old Capulet does for Juliet, or Touchstone for his daughter in the play of *Eastward Ho* (1605). Nor, having arranged it, would he usually expect to receive this answer: 'Sir, I am all yours: your body gave me life: your care and love, happiness and life: let your virtues still direct it, for to your wisdom I wholly dispose myself.' In Shakespeare's time such notions were commonly associated with the words 'king', 'daughter', and 'father'.

In another direction modern scholarship has been profoundly affected by a renewed interest in the study of early texts. The most stimulating pioneer work here was by A. W. Pollard. In *Shakespeare's Fight with the Pirates* (1917) he showed that some of the earliest of Shakespeare's texts were often set up directly from Shakespeare's own manuscript by a printer who followed his copy closely. This, at the time, was a revolutionary idea, for when Bradley produced his lectures it was generally felt that the Shakespearean text had been established and was unalterable. Generations of editors from the early eighteenth century onwards had edited Shakespeare's texts, emending difficult passages and formalizing them, so that the Globe or Cambridge text was regarded as the 'authorized version' of Shakespeare. Now the new and

* For the whole speech, see pp. 199–203.

exact study of bibliography, exemplified in McKerrow's edition
of Nashe, showed that there was a wealth of interest in the detailed comparison and examination of early texts. The result was
that when scholars again began to look at the early Quarto and
Folio texts with respectful interest, and not merely to despise
them as the semi-illiterate efforts of bungling printers, all kinds
of new discoveries were made.

It is indeed a revelation to read a familiar play for the first
time in a Quarto or Folio text. The reader finds himself at once
in the atmosphere of the Globe Theatre. Most plays in the original
texts have no scene divisions; many even have no act divisions.
There are none of those place headings which editors have added –
Act I, Scene i, *A Room in the Palace*; Act IV, Scene iii, *Another
Part of the Field*. These were not noted in the original text because
in the Elizabethan theatre there was no scenery and little physical
indication of a change of locality. The reader realizes at once how
editors have tampered with the original texts, sometimes by
brilliant guessing producing sense from corrupt passages, but
more commonly by erecting an eighteenth-century façade to an
Elizabethan play.

Antony and Cleopatra is an extreme example of editorial
method. The play is sometimes criticized because there are too
many scenes. Thus, in the Fourth Act there are, according to the
Globe text, no less than thirteen scenes:

i	*Before Alexandria. Caesar's Camp.*
ii	*Alexandria. A room in the Palace.*
iii	*The Same. Before the Palace.*
iv	*The Same. A room in the Palace.*
v	*Alexandria. Antony's Camp.*
vi	*Before Alexandria. Caesar's Camp.*
vii	*Field of Battle between the Camps.*
viii	*Under the Walls of Alexandria.*
ix	*Caesar's Camp.*
x	*Between the two Camps.*

In the Folio text there are no scene divisions at all.

The old editorial principle was that when all characters have gone off the stage a scene ends. A scene must take place somewhere. Therefore the place must be indicated. But in Shakespeare's play, as originally intended for the stage, scenes were not *place-scenes* but rather *person-scenes*, and here at the crisis of the fortunes of Antony, Caesar, and Cleopatra, Shakespeare shows how each rises or declines at the supreme moment. In the Folio text there are therefore no scene divisions, no place headings. The scenes, in fact, are concerned with Caesar: Antony and Cleopatra: the common soldiers: Antony and Cleopatra: Antony: Caesar: the battle: Antony and Cleopatra: Enobarbus: the defeat of Antony: Cleopatra hearing the news: Antony's attempt to stab himself: Cleopatra's distress: Antony's death. Such a dramatic technique can be understood only when we remember that the play is Elizabethan and written for an Elizabethan stage. If Act IV is split into thirteen different localities, then the attention of the reader or spectator is distracted from the persons to the place, and the play becomes unreadable and unactable.

Another offence of editors of the eighteenth and nineteenth centuries was that they tampered with the punctuation and the arrangement of the lines. Often they were justified, but their enthusiasm was excessive. Percy Simpson, in a little book called *Shakespearean Punctuation* (1911) first pointed out that the punctuation in the First Folio was dramatic and not grammatical. In the Folio especially, and the Quartos far more casually, the texts were punctuated for recitation. The punctuation is not always consistent or sound, and it is very doubtful if Shakespeare was responsible for it; but certainly the punctuation is contemporary and inserted by those who knew and did their business well. Later editors, by normalizing Shakespearean punctuation to modern

grammatical usage, have wiped out many of the original subtleties.
In the best Folio texts we are not only in imagination in the
Globe Theatre but can also hear the speeches spoken as Shake-
speare's actors delivered them.

Some examples will make this clear. The opening lines of
Twelfth Night in the accepted text are punctuated thus:

> If music be the food of love, play on;
> Give me excess of it, that, surfeiting,
> The appetite may sicken, and so die.
> That strain again! It had a dying fall:
> O! it came o'er mine ear like the sweet sound
> That breathes upon a bank of violets,
> Stealing and giving odour.

In the Folio these lines are punctuated:

> If Music be the food of Love, play on,
> Give me excess of it: that surfeiting,
> The appetite may sicken, and so die.
> That strain again, it had a dying fall:
> O, it came o'er my ear, like the sweet sound
> That breathes upon a bank of Violets;
> Stealing, and giving Odour.

Antony's speech over Caesar's corpse is punctuated in the
accepted text:

> Friends, Romans, countrymen, lend me your ears;
> I come to bury Caesar, not to praise him.
> The evil that men do lives after them,
> The good is oft interred with their bones;
> So let it be with Caesar. The noble Brutus
> Hath told you Caesar was ambitious;
> If it were so, it was a grievous fault,
> And grievously hath Caesar answer'd it.
> Here, under leave of Brutus and the rest, –
> For Brutus is an honourable man;

So are they all, all honourable men, –
Come I to speak in Caesar's funeral.
He was my friend, faithful and just to me:
But Brutus says he was ambitious;
And Brutus is an honourable man.
He hath brought many captives home to Rome,
Whose ransoms did the general coffers fill:
Did this in Caesar seem ambitious?
When that the poor have cried, Caesar hath wept;
Ambition should be made of sterner stuff:
Yet Brutus says he was ambitious:
And Brutus is an honourable man.
You all did see that on the Lupercal
I thrice presented him a kingly crown,
Which he did thrice refuse: was this ambition?
Yet Brutus says he was ambitious;
And, sure, he is an honourable man.
I speak not to disprove what Brutus spoke,
But here I am to speak what I do know.
You all did love him once, not without cause:
What cause withholds you then to mourn for him?
O judgement! thou art fled to brutish beasts,
And men have lost their reason. Bear with me;
My heart is in the coffin there with Caesar,
And I must pause till it come back to me.

In the Folio text the punctuation of the speech runs thus:

Friends, Romans, Countrymen, lend me your ears:
I come to bury Caesar, not to praise him:
The evil that men do, lives after them,
The good is oft interred with their bones,
So let it be with Caesar. The Noble Brutus,
Hath told you Caesar was Ambitious:
If it were so, it was a grievous fault,
And grievously hath Caesar answer'd it.
Here, under leave of Brutus, and the rest
(For Brutus is an Honourable man,

became the source of authority in all matters of doctrine, interpretation of the Scriptures, discipline, and morals. Further, he was persuaded by his then minister, Thomas Cromwell, to 'dissolve' (as the historians euphemistically call it) the religious houses and to seize their vast wealth. But the loot was not used for charitable purposes; the social charities, such as schools and hospitals for the poor, mostly disappeared. Nor was it used to strengthen the Crown. Most of it was acquired by the friends and followers of Cromwell.

The changes caused by the upheaval were disastrous. The new rich were demoralized by sudden chances of vast unearned wealth. The poor suffered most because in the general grab they were victims of enclosures and exploitation. It took several generations before a new stability was established. In many ways, though the parallels should not be pushed too closely, the English revolution of the first half of the sixteenth century was comparable to the Nazi and Communist revolutions in the twentieth century.

In breaking with Rome, Henry VIII had not intended to transform England into a Protestant country but rather to maintain a Catholic Church without the Pope. Henry VIII was succeeded by his young son, Edward VI, a boy of nine, who was dominated by guardians who had benefited from the spoils of the religious houses and were thus hot partisans of the new religion. Apart from doctrinal changes, the Reformation under Edward VI was the worst artistic disaster which ever happened in England. Everywhere the ornaments of the Church – statues, vestments, sacred vessels, mural paintings, stained glass, illuminated manuscripts, books – were destroyed wholesale. Moreover the demand for such works of art suddenly ceased and the traditions of generations of craftsmen were lost. Edward reigned for five years; for the next five years (1553–8) there was a Catholic reaction under his sister, Mary; finally in 1558, a second Protestant Reformation under Elizabeth I.

These revolutions also meant that England was cut off from

the civilized countries of Catholic Europe – Italy, France, and Spain – so that England became an Iron Curtain country, suspected by her neighbours, and not unreasonably, for English embassies in Catholic countries were centres of anti-Catholic (that is, revolutionary) propaganda.

For the individual the upheavals were as disturbing. For a thousand years men had been brought up to respect the authority, teaching, and moral order of the Catholic Church. Now, within a generation, they learnt drastically and brutally that the dictator and not the Church was the first and last word in belief and moral conduct. The result was that the English, who had been the most religious race in Europe, ceased to be interested in religion, except for small parties of zealots, but, as usually happens, the heroic and willing martyrs were a small minority. Most men accepted the established order, and the more willingly because they realized that Elizabeth was the last of her line; she had no certain heir, and it was only too likely that her death would be followed by another period of disputed succession, civil war, and general anarchy. This grim prospect was a constant anxiety of statesmen through the reign; it is subtly present in each of Shakespeare's History plays.

Shakespeare's father grew up during the years of change. His sympathies, it seems clear, were with the old and not with the new order. By the time Shakespeare became conscious of what was happening around him, the new order was firmly established. His generation, like the generation of the 1960s in Soviet Russia, had been nurtured on the current myths, one of which was that the Prince was semi-divine. He was God's direct and immediate representative on earth. Queen Elizabeth in one of her proclamations declared: 'Forasmuch as it is manifestly seen to all the world how it hath pleased Almighty God of His Most Singular favour to have taken this Our Realm into His Special Protection these many years even from the beginning of our Reign . . . with special preservation of Our Own Person as next under His

Almightiness, Supreme Governor of the same.' Shakespeare him-self – if he wrote the famous passage in the play of Sir Thomas More – expressed the theory even more eloquently (see p. 202). There are certain political advantages in such an attitude, pro-vided that the Supreme Governor is expert in the art of govern-ment, as Elizabeth I certainly was.

The age of Shakespeare was thus uneasy, even if generous-minded historians call it the 'age of the "Renaissance"', the 'age of the emancipation of the individual' from ancient bondage. Individual Englishmen, however, were less conscious of emanci-pation than of the dangers of failing to conform to the official pattern of conduct and thought. Attendance at the services of the Established Church of England was compulsory. Those who chose to obey their own consciences – Catholics and to a lesser extent Puritans – were brutally punished by fines, imprisonment, torture, and execution.

Moreover, the moral and psychological support once given by the Church was destroyed. Before the Reformation, a man in-volved in personal and psychological problems could find relief in confession and absolution. Now confession to a priest was abolished – and psychiatry had not yet been established. Hamlet with his broodings over man and the universe was a typical example of the intellectual, trying to reconstruct from broken fragments a new moral order.

Nevertheless there was gain as well as loss. Having rejected the teaching of the Church, the more enlightened of the reformers looked to education, which meant the study of the classics of Greece and Rome, as the way of salvation. Learning began with the training in languages given to boys in the grammar schools, about which, as it happens, there is much information.

At Westminster, for instance, school started early. At six in the morning the boys stood round their master repeating by heart eight or ten pages from Lily's *Latin Grammar*. They made verses in Latin or Greek, extempore, on some given theme. They expounded some passages from Cicero, Livy, Isocrates, Homer, Apollonius, Xenophon. After this they adjourned for breakfast. At nine work prepared overnight was heard. Then they practised *dictamina* – extempore translation into Latin or Greek of some sentences (in the Elizabethan sense – gems of wisdom or proverbs such as delighted the heart of Polonius). Next the master himself expounded some part of a classic in prose or verse which the boys were expected to be able to repeat in the afternoon when they went through the passage, construing its grammatical parts, admiring the rhetorical figures, or turning it from prose to verse or verse to prose. And, inevitably, they learnt it by heart for regurgitation in the morning. The training was not all so sterile or mechanical as it sounds, for if the tree is to be judged by its fruits, then Shakespeare's generation would seem to have profited by its schooling. It taught a boy, and subsequently a man, to develop and use his memory; it gave him a fine appreciation for language, read and heard. Shakespeare wrote as he did, not only because he was taught the arts of language at school, but because he had audiences who keenly appreciated the finest speech, prose and verse.

Nor was the Elizabethan training in Latin and Greek confined to the language. No one can read the great classics – Virgil, Livy, Cicero, Homer, Caesar, Sallust, Demosthenes, Thucydides, or Xenophon – without achieving some kind of insight into history, moral law, philosophy, civics, psychology, and sociology. The Elizabethans had the keenest interest in these matters which were not first discovered in the twentieth century. They recognized, and stressed, that history was the record of moral law at work. This is the grand theme of Shakespeare's History Plays; and here, as usual, he is not the unique exception but the reflection of a common interest.

Shakespeare's History Plays thus meant far more to his first audiences than they can to us, for they dealt with events which were still important. Moreover, when the totalitarian state suppresses free comment on the present, the re-creation of the past can often be consoling. Elizabeth's Privy Council was hyper-sensitive about history, and so greatly embarrassed by certain historical parallels which were being made, that in June 1599 – midway in Shakespeare's career – they forbade all plays of English History. It was probably not a coincidence that Shakespeare's next play was the Roman tragedy of *Julius Caesar*.

The London theatre was the only place where the common man could hear direct and honest comment on life. Players, said Hamlet, are the abstract and brief chronicles of the time. That also was the view of Queen Elizabeth; and the history of the theatres shows that every few months a sensitive Government peremptorily commanded them to be shut. Too saucy a play got the author into trouble. Ben Jonson was in trouble at least four times for taking liberties. When Essex's followers were plotting their rebellion in February 1601, they bribed Shakespeare's Company to play *Richard the Second* as part of their propaganda, for that play showed how a Sovereign, who was surrounded by favourites, was overthrown and deposed by one whom he had wronged. Two years later, when the Queen was dying, the first step taken to guard against disorder was to shut the playhouses.

The Elizabethan therefore went to the theatre with his ears open and his wits keen to detect hidden meanings.

While Shakespeare's History Plays presented men in political societies, his Comedies and his Tragedies dealt rather with man as a social unit. We need therefore some knowledge of how society was organized and what conventions of behaviour were regarded as normal.

At the top of the pyramid was the Sovereign, enshrined in a ritual which expressed the divinity of kings. To the ordinary person the Queen was inaccessible. Privy Councillors had the right of access, but few others; and even they were expected to converse with her on their knees, unless invited as a special mark of favour to stand. Small wonder that the poets of that age competed in offering their tributes (which sometimes seem so silly) to Eliza the Faery Queen. Shakespeare seldom joined in that chorus, for the often quoted remark in *A Midsummer Night's Dream* is exceptional:

> Cupid all armed . . .
>   a certain aim he took
> At a fair Vestal, throned by the west,
> And loos'd his love-shaft smartly from his bow,
> As it should pierce a hundred thousand hearts:
> But I might see young Cupid's fiery shaft
> Quench'd in the chaste beams of the watery Moon;
> And the imperial Votaress passed on,
> In maiden meditation, fancy-free.   (II, i, 156)

When this tribute was written, the Royal Vestal was aged sixty-one.

In *Richard the Second*, Shakespeare put into the mouth of the Bishop of Carlisle a most stirring speech about the divinity of kings, and earlier Richard himself had declared

> Not all the water in the rough rude sea
> Can wash the balm off from an anointed King.

But this was grim ironical prelude to the unkinging of Richard in the Fourth Act. Kings in their office might be divine; in their persons they were usually too too human. At the same time Shakespeare realized that behind the pomp lay the lonely awful responsibility; and he expressed it most feelingly in Henry V's moving soliloquy on the vanity of kingly pomp (IV, i, 246).

Next to the sovereign in the social order came the nobility. Shakespeare and his fellows had ample knowledge of the haughty insolence of noblemen, for players depended for their existence on the favour of their Lord whose licence was their sole protection against mayors and other enemies of the drama. Noblemen were created as a special mark of favour by a patent bestowed by the Sovereign and sealed with the Great Seal of England. They were beings apart and treated with a ceremony less but similar to that used toward the Queen. They had great estates and many servants but also great responsibilities for they were expected to serve the state at their own expense as ambassadors extraordinary, generals in the field, members of the Upper House of Parliament, and – most expensive of all – as hosts to the Queen when she made her summer progress. It is, however, false romanticism to regard the Elizabethan nobility as all descended from those who came over with William the Conqueror; many of them owed their position to speculations in monastic land made by their fathers and grandfathers.

Next to the nobility in the chain of order came the knights and gentlemen. A man was made knight by the Sovereign in person or by her deputy, such as the general on a campaign. Queen Elizabeth was very sparing in her knighthoods; and it was one of the major causes of her anger with Essex that he was far too generous in bestowing knighthoods when he was in command of her armies. When King James came to the English throne, he was so lavish with knighthoods – he made 900 knights in his first year – that the title became a joke.

Next came the gentlemen. Legally a gentleman was a man of good birth and independent means who was not employed in a gainful profession. Accordingly he was expected to serve his poorer neighbours with public duties, as magistrate, member of Parliament, or on one of the many local committees. In theory also a man who made his money in trade or by using his hands was not a gentleman because he was concerned with enriching himself not with serving the community. Officially, a gentleman was one to whom the College of Heralds had granted a coat of arms; but in fact a sufficient income has always been the most important mark of an English gentleman. Shakespeare himself qualified as a gentleman when in 1596 a grant of arms was made to his father; but there were some who sneered that players were not fit persons to be included in the ranks of the gentlemen.

As for the unnumbered poor, they were very poor, and their

standard of living was very low. A skilled workman in the City of London earned 10d. to 14d. a day. Food at first sight was much cheaper; butter sold at 4d. a lb. and eggs at 7 for 2d., but 2d. was the wage for 2 hours work. Clothing was far more expensive. Rents were comparatively cheap and servants could be hired for very low wages.

Family life was far more important than today. Most men and women lived and died in the same town or village where they had been born. The father was the head of the family and its ruler. His absolute right to dispose of his daughters in marriage was indeed questioned but the picture of the Capulet family is not far from the fact. In his own eyes Old Capulet is a considerate father. When the question of Juliet marrying Paris is first discussed, he is willing at least to let the girl have the choice of refusing; it is not until she becomes impudent that he issues commands.

In Shakespeare's plays there is little trace of any real understanding between the generations or of family affection. Polonius and Brabantio have small regard for their daughters. Even Prospero, though certainly fond of Miranda, is hardly a companionable father; and Lear for all his deep love for Cordelia has to learn a bitter lesson before their love has any kind of equality. Children were brought up to fear and respect their parents, and to show it by their attitude. A son called his father 'Sir' and stood in his presence. The power, might, and authority of the father were thus recognized as part of the social order.

As for women, they had few rights of their own. On marriage, a woman's goods and money passed into the possession of her husband unless special settlements were made by the lawyers. Any woman with money thus had ample choice of a husband; and there were many scandals in real life, especially as a binding contract was so simple. It was necessary only for a man and a woman to declare verbally before two witnesses that they took each other as man and wife for the contract to be binding, so that either party could claim fulfilment and prevent the marriage of the other to a third party. Nor was it difficult for an unscrupulous fortune-hunter to produce perjured witnesses of a verbal contract. The religious ceremony was but the public confirmation of a plight already made and sometimes fulfilled.

One notorious case was made the subject of a play by Chapman.* A girl called Agnes Howe was left a large fortune by her aunt. Immediately suitors began to make handsome offers to her parents, who were poor and not too honest. Before long no less than four men came forward and declared that they were legally betrothed to Agnes (and her money). The father was in distress, as each prepared to go to law to enforce his claim. He therefore turned to his minister, the Rev. Thomas Milward, who solved the problem by marrying the girl himself, but with such irregularity that he was in trouble with the ecclesiastical authorities. It took four years of cross lawsuits before the minister was finally able to claim Agnes, and what was left of her fortune, as his very own. At no time did the Courts ask Agnes which of her suitors she had regarded as her true husband. It was also noted by gossips that on an occasion when the minister was preaching at Paul's Cross, a cuckoo flew over the pulpit crying out 'Cuckoo, cuckoo'; but the cuckoo is a scandalous bird.

This power of betrothal is central to Shakespeare's *Measure for Measure* when the Duke disguised as a friar tells Mariana that she has every right to obtain Angelo by a midnight assignation. His knowledge of moral theology is, however, very weak.

Elizabethan widows with property were always in danger from fortune hunters and they seldom remained single for long. Though Hamlet's disgust is understandable, his mother was but following common custom in remarrying before the funeral bakemeats were quite cold. There was an etiquette in the matter; a widow could not decently accept a proposal of remarriage so long as the corpse of her late husband was still in the house.

* Discovered and detailed by C. J. Sisson in *Lost Plays of Shakespeare's Age*, 1936.

While some of the true records of marriage are quite horrible, sometimes the ending was as happy as in any Elizabethan comedy. Such was the story of Elizabeth Spencer.

In the latter years of Queen Elizabeth, one of the richest men in London was Alderman Sir John Spencer. He had an only daughter called Elizabeth. Naturally she had many suitors, but she was obstinate and so exasperated her father that he beat her soundly and shut her up for falling in love with one of whom he did not approve – the young Lord Compton. Elizabeth was furious and told her lover who made trouble, with the result that Sir John was for a while imprisoned for ill-treating his daughter. Relations at home thus became very strained.

But Lord Compton was a man of spirit. One day he disguised himself as the baker's man and arrived at Sir John's house carrying on his back the great basket of bread for the household. Having delivered the bread he went out with the basket – and Elizabeth inside. They were married. Sir John retorted by disinheriting his daughter. In due time Elizabeth gave birth to a son, but still Sir John refused to relent. The young couple took their trouble to the old Queen, whom one does not often associate with such romantic episodes. She sent a message to Sir John that she was to be gossip – godmother – to an infant in whom she was especially interested, and she invited him to be the other godparent. Sir John was much flattered and when the Queen named the child 'Spencer' he was delighted; since he had disinherited his daughter, he would make this child his heir. Thereupon the young couple stepped out from behind the arras and begged for forgiveness, and there was general reconciliation.

Not many years afterwards, Sir John died leaving a fortune of £300,000 in money of that day – an enormous fortune. Lord Compton was so excited that for a while he went off his head; but he soon recovered, and in time he became a great nobleman.

Another romantic match was made by Robert Dudley, only son of the great Earl of Leicester, Queen Elizabeth's contemporary and favourite in earlier days. Dudley's legitimacy was doubtful. His mother declared that she was married to Leicester who retorted that she was mistaken. The son naturally claimed legitimacy but in 1605 the Star Chamber decision went against him. Soon afterwards he went abroad with Elizabeth Southwell who had been Maid of Honour to Queen Elizabeth, and when they eloped she disguised herself as his page.

The most famous of all Elizabethan romances is the marriage of John Donne and Anne More. Donne in his twenties was a young man of great promise, well on the way to high office in the State as secretary to Sir Thomas Egerton. Up to 1601, he was notorious for his love affairs with ladies of society. Then for the first time he fell in love – true love – with the young niece of his employer, and they were secretly married. But secret marriage was so contrary to accepted ideas, especially in high society, that the angry father caused bridegroom, best man, and minister to be imprisoned. As a result Donne's career was ruined and for eight years he and his wife lived in great poverty until her father relented.

But even in Shakespeare's age there were normal happy marriages. Edward Alleyn, the great actor, married Joan Woodward, stepdaughter of Phillip Henslowe, in 1592. Ten years after the marriage, Alleyn was away in the country, and Joan wrote to send him the news. The plague was hot in London. She began:

'My entire and well-beloved sweetheart. Still it joys me and long I pray God may I joy to hear of your health and welfare as you of ours. Almighty God be thanked my own self yourself' – a pretty thought, 'you are me and I am you'; one expects that kind of sentiment from John Donne but hardly in an ordinary letter of home chat – 'and my mother and whole house is in good health.' Then she gives him the local news: the plague is very bad; Old Brown of the Boar's Head is dead and died very poor, and father is at Court; and as for his coming home, he is to use his discretion – 'let it not be as I will, but at your own best liking.

I am glad to hear you take delight in hawking, though you have worn your apparel to rags. The best is you know where to have better. And as welcome to me shall be with your rags as if you were in cloth of gold or velvet. Try and see . . . And so sweetheart, once more farewell till we meet, which I hope shall not be long.'*

There was not much wrong with that marriage. It is a mistake to suppose that every Elizabethan husband was a brute or a cuckold, and every wife either a trodden worm, a wanton, or a shrew. History is the record of the abnormal, not of the day-to-day decencies of home life, just as drama to be dramatic portrays the unusual, even in comedy. Shakespeare's plays are seldom pictures of life as it was in the sixteenth century.

Nevertheless the marriages of Alleyn and of Donne were curiously linked. Rather more than twenty years after his marriage, Donne was a widower with a large family, but also a leading figure in the Anglican Church. He was now Dean of St Paul's and a famous preacher. His eldest daughter Catherine needed a husband; unlike her mother she left the choice to her father. Dean Donne bargained for a suitable young man, but the arrangement fell through. At this moment a new suitor appeared – old Edward Alleyn. He had just lost his faithful Joan and he was very disconsolate; but not for long. He met Catherine Donne at dinner and made an offer to the Dean. After some hard bargaining, Catherine became the second Mrs Alleyn, and for the next three years Alleyn quarrelled continuously with his new father-in-law (who was nine years younger) because Donne failed to fulfil his side of the bargain. Then Alleyn died leaving his dear and loving wife £100 and her own jewellery. Naturally she married again and a man nearer her own age.

Many other matters affected Shakespeare's audiences and are reflected in his plays. There is a popular fallacy that the reign of Elizabeth I was, apart from the Spanish Armada of 1588, a time

* *Henslowe Papers*, p. 59.

of peace and smiling plenty. Actually the first half of Shakespeare's working life·– from the beginning to *Hamlet* and *Othello* – was overshadowed by a war which seemed interminable.

The year after the Armada – 1589 – Drake was sent to Portugal with a large force. That expedition failed, for although Lisbon and Corunna were sacked, there were heavy losses by disease. In 1590, English soldiers were aiding the Dutch against the Spanish King. In 1591, two small English expeditions were fighting in Brittany and Normandy. Here the young Earl of Essex had first experience in command and was led to suppose that he was destined to become a great general – an illusion that ultimately led to his downfall. In 1594, a second expedition to Brittany captured Brest. In 1595, there was the greatest alarm; a new Spanish Armada was preparing and the Spaniards were not likely to repeat the mistakes of '88. The expedition came to nothing for disease broke out among the Spanish soldiers.

In 1596, a great English fleet was collected – as great as that which fought off the Armada. It was still preparing when the Spaniards suddenly surrounded Calais. Essex at this time was at Dover supervising the assembly of the ships. He begged to be allowed to go over with such troops as could be mustered; but the Queen, as so often, vacillated. First she ordered that the troops should be assembled; and then the order was countermanded. Two days later the Lord Mayor of London and his officers were again directed to muster all available troops. It was Easter Sunday and the people were making their Easter communion. The constables shut the church doors until they had collected the necessary men. Four days later the rumble of cannon could be heard all day in London; and then there was silence. Calais had fallen.

So the preparations went forward, and in June the great fleet sailed. They occupied Cadiz with very little opposition, stayed there for three weeks, burnt a great Spanish merchant fleet, sacked the town and came home with very little loss. The 'Cadiz Voyage' was a brilliant success, and great loot was collected; but the

Queen was much dissatisfied for her share was small; the soldiers and sailors had made off with all portable plunder.

In 1597, another expedition was prepared (known later as the Islands Voyage), intended to repeat the success of 1596, but the weather was bad all that summer, and instead of attacking Spain they made for the Azores Islands to wait for the Spanish treasure fleet. But the expedition was a failure for there was constant bickering between the soldiers and the sailors. When the ships came home – in no kind of order or discipline – England was in a state of panic. Another Spanish Armada was reported at sea; but as in '88 the storms were too much for them and none of the ships reached England. It was at this time that Shakespeare's *1 Henry IV* was first played to audiences largely of returned soldiers, and Falstaff and his gang first appeared on the stage.

The war with Spain languished in 1598, but in Ireland the situation suddenly became desperate. The Irish rose under Hugh O'Neil, Earl of Tyrone, slaughtered most of the English garrison, and for a while it seemed that Ireland would be lost. In this rising Edmund Spenser was forced to run for his life; he died soon after of the hardships he had suffered.

In 1599 Essex was sent to Ireland with the largest and best-equipped army that left England during the reign – an event to which Shakespeare refers in *Henry V* (v, Prologue, 30). Essex failed miserably and by September he was back in England in disgrace. He never recovered the favour of the Queen, and eighteen months later he made his futile rebellion.

In 1600, there was war on two fronts. English troops were aiding the Dutch, and in Ireland Lord Mountjoy was trying to restore order. The war was at its worst in 1601, though at the end of the year the tide turned and decisive victories in both fields offered some hope of an end to the troubles. The war with Spain came finally to an end in 1603 when the old Queen died. Wars were the personal quarrels of sovereigns; and her successor, James of Scotland, was at peace with Spain.

War thus touched everyone. There was a continual demand for soldiers from the City and the counties, and money had to be raised by special taxes. Several of the most famous writers had first-hand experience of campaigning. Donne, Spenser, Campion, Lodge, Jonson all served at some time. Small wonder that there are so many soldier characters in Shakespeare's plays, and of all types and ranks. Generals such as Othello, Henry V, and Coriolanus; commanders in plenty in the History Plays; doughty fighters such as Hotspur and Hector; competent company commanders as Fluellen and Gower; and the unscrupulous rogues who pester every army – Falstaff, Pistol, Parolles, Bardolph, and the rest. There is no record that Shakespeare was ever a soldier in his earlier manhood; but he certainly had a knowledge of soldiers and their ways which is far beyond that which comes to most civilians.

Queen Elizabeth died in the early hours of 24 March 1603, having reigned 44 years and 5 months. 'About 10 o'clock,' noted the Lady Anne Clifford in her diary, 'King James was proclaimed in Cheapside by all the Council with great joy and triumph. I went to see and hear. This peaceable coming in of the King was unexpected of all sorts of people.' Similarly Sir Roger Wilbraham recorded the Queen's death in his journal 'whereupon the people both in city and counties, finding the just fear of 40 years for want of a known successor dissolved in a minute, did so rejoice as few wished the gracious Queen alive again.'

The Queen's death was in many ways the end of an age. Though it is customary to regard Shakespeare as primarily an 'Elizabethan', actually the greatest of his plays were written for the pleasure of King James I, who was a far more enthusiastic patron of the drama than his predecessor.

The coming of the new King brought changes to others beside his new players and his now unemployed soldiers. For the first

20 The Head of Queen Elizabeth I: a monument in Westminster Abbey

time since Henry VIII, there was a royal family at Court, and royal children – young Henry, the Hope of England, Elizabeth, a real fairy princess who inherited the charm of her grandmother Mary Queen of Scots, and little Charles, an undersized backward boy.

But James, though a man of considerable learning and real intelligence (for which he seldom gets credit), was not well suited to play the part of God's Immediate Deputy on Earth. To be successful a dictator needs certain qualities: a personal dignity, and a presence that inspires fear in his servants. James did not possess these gifts and his Court life and public administration soon degenerated. There had been scandals in the Court of Elizabeth, but at least there was outward decorum, and official salaries were punctually paid. Under James the old restraints soon broke down and the scandals at Court were unseemly and outrageous.

There is a famous account of the goings-on in the summer of 1606 when James entertained his royal brother-in-law, the King of Denmark, on a state visit. Hamlet had some hard remarks about the drunkenness of the Danes; that judgement was amply illustrated. The worst and most memorable occasion was when Robert Cecil, now Earl of Salisbury, entertained the two Kings at Theobalds with a symbolic Masque of the visit of the Queen of Sheba to King Solomon.

The lady playing the Queen of Sheba was so drunk that in coming up to his Danish Majesty she tripped over the stairs and upset a tray of wines, jellies, and cream into the royal lap. When the King had been mopped up, he rose and attempted to dance, but he fell down and was carried off to bed. Other ladies enacting Faith, Hope, and Charity were in a like condition, and were led away protesting to sleep, or to quarrel, or to vomit in the outer Hall.

Shakespeare and his Company were among those who contributed to the entertainments, and they heard the disgusted comments of the older courtiers. It is hardly surprising that in the later plays of Shakespeare and others there should be found a feeling, fairly often expressed, that Court life was essentially rotten, and a nostalgic desire to escape into the country.

But an age should not be judged solely by its noisier scandals. In many families there was a graciousness of living not seen before, and seldom since, as in the home life of John Milton with his parents (but not, it may be added, in the home life of Milton with his own wives or children), or of George Herbert and his mother, or in the praises of childhood in the writings of Vaughan, Traherne, or Earle, all of whom were raised in the first quarter of the seventeenth century.

A knowledge and understanding of the social and historical background adds vastly to the immediate and remote enjoyment of Shakespeare's plays. We learn to see and to read them with the understanding of a contemporary. It does more; it adds to our understanding of humanity. There are many other ways of studying Shakespeare. A great artist transcends his own generation. Nevertheless the nearer we can come to Shakespeare in his own times, the fuller our enjoyment of what he wrote.

5

Shakespeare's Company

The company of actors known first as the Lord Chamberlain's Players, and later as the King's Men, came into existence in the summer of 1594. There had been severe outbreaks of the plague in 1592 and 1593, and at such times the London playhouses were closed. The companies were badly disorganized by these continual interruptions. When at last playing could be resumed in London, there was a considerable regrouping. Edward Alleyn, now at the peak of his fame as an actor of tragedy parts, formed a new company under the patronage of the Lord Admiral, which opened at the Rose Theatre. A few weeks later a new Lord Chamberlain's Company began to play at the Theatre at Shoreditch, north of the city. This playhouse was owned by James Burbage.

The Theatre had been built in 1576. In the 1570s there was much friction between the playing companies and the Lord Mayor and Aldermen of the City of London. Hitherto, players had acted for the public in various City inns. It was not a desirable arrangement, and the City authorities did their utmost to prevent it. Their objections to plays were those common to any form of public entertainment which attracts rowdy crowds. Plays sometimes caused riots and disturbances and the players indulged in unseemly comment on their betters. Above all, there was a perpetual risk of the plague, which was easily spread in crowded assemblies. The Lord Mayor succeeded in preventing the players from acting within the jurisdiction of the City; the legal boundaries of the City, however, were small, and London was already spreading out well beyond its limits. To the north in the Middlesex suburbs, and south of the river in the Surrey suburbs, jurisdiction lay with the magistrates of Middlesex and Surrey, who were far more complacent.

In 1576 James Burbage acquired a twenty-one years' lease of a piece of land in Shoreditch, north of the City, and there erected the first permanent playhouse, which was named the Theatre. The venture was a success. Other playhouses followed. By 1594, there were also the Curtain in the Shoreditch neighbourhood, and the Rose on the Bankside, the suburb which had grown up at the south end of London Bridge.

James Burbage had originally been chief player of the great Earl of Leicester. His son, Richard Burbage (born *c.* 1568), was now making a name for himself as a tragic actor. He learnt his business under Alleyn, but they parted company; and now, in the autumn of 1594, Richard Burbage became the leader of a new Lord Chamberlain's Company. This Company also included Will Kempe,* and Shakespeare.

Marlowe and Greene, hitherto the only English writers to make much name for themselves on the public stage, were now dead. Kyd, the author of the famous *Spanish Tragedy*, died before the end of 1594. Thus, for a few months, the Chamberlain's Men had a great advantage in Shakespeare, who was the only dramatist with any considerable reputation.

By 1594 Shakespeare had already written the three parts of *Henry VI*, and *Richard III*, which told the story of the beginnings of the Wars of the Roses and their final end, when Henry Tudor defeated Richard III at the Battle of Bosworth Field, and *Titus Andronicus*, *The Two Gentlemen of Verona*, *Love's Labour's Lost*, *The Taming of the Shrew*, and *The Comedy of Errors*.

The Lord Chamberlain's Company acted *The Comedy of*

* See p. 150.

Errors at Christmas 1594, as part of the elaborate revels put on by the young gentlemen of Gray's Inn at Court. One of their earliest successes was *Romeo and Juliet*, which perfectly accorded with the mood of the moment for sonneteering and love poetry. Soon afterwards Shakespeare wrote *A Midsummer Night's Dream*, apparently for some special performance at a wedding, and about 1595 he continued the story of the troubles of the fifteenth century, by showing how they all began when Richard II was unlawfully deposed, and afterwards murdered by his cousin, Henry Bolingbroke, thereby bringing down the curse upon the House of Lancaster which was the theme of the plays of the Wars of the Roses. *King John* and *The Merchant of Venice* were written probably in 1596.

The Company had its disappointments in 1596. James Burbage, who in his own way had a touch of genius, realized that conditions in the playgoing world were changing. In the 1580s men of taste and education had little good to say of the theatres. Sir Philip Sidney, in his *Apology for Poetry*, condemned playwrights heartily for their lack of propriety. Now, however, good writers had been attracted to write for professional players, and young men of fashion and intelligence were becoming interested in the theatre. Burbage saw that they, rather than the general public, were the most paying patrons of the theatre. But gentlemen of taste were put off by the mixed and noisy crowds who paid their pennies to stand in the yard of the public playhouse. In the 1580s a very successful private theatre existed for a few years in Blackfriars. It had been managed by John Lyly and the actors were choirboys from St Paul's and the Chapel Royal. Lyly's venture came to an end about 1590. While it lasted it catered solely for a better-class audience.

James Burbage thought to revive the idea of the private theatre. Plays in the public theatres were acted in the open air. A private indoor theatre would not be affected by the weather, and it was better to attract a small audience paying good prices than a larger audience paying their pennies. He therefore acquired the refectory of the old Blackfriars Monastery – the site is now occupied by the *Times* building – and proceeded at considerable expense to turn it into an indoor playhouse.

Blackfriars at this time was a fashionable residential quarter. The aristocratic inhabitants complained that the playhouse would be a great nuisance with its noises of drums and trumpets, and its crowds of people. Accordingly the Privy Council gave orders that Burbage was not to use the building for playing, and the venture was for a long time a complete loss. Soon afterwards, James Burbage died.

The year 1597 also was full of anxiety for the Lord Chamberlain's Men. The lease of the ground upon which the Theatre stood had originally been taken out for twenty-one years. By the conditions of the lease, which expired in April 1597, either Burbage could renew the lease on agreed terms, or he must remove the playhouse building before its expiry. If he did not fulfil these conditions then the building was appropriated to the ground landlord, a man called Giles Alleyn. Alleyn proved difficult. He knew that the players wished to retain their theatre, but he refused to offer terms which were in any way acceptable. The wrangle continued for many months.

Meanwhile, on 28 July 1597, all theatres were peremptorily shut by order of the Privy Council. The trouble arose through the Earl of Pembroke's players, who were playing at the Swan (a new playhouse erected on the Bankside) where they put on a seditious and topical comedy called *The Isle of Dogs*, written by Thomas Nashe and Ben Jonson. Jonson at this time was an actor in Pembroke's Company. The Privy Council were so angry that they ordered playing to cease forthwith, and Jonson and two fellow-actors, Gabriel Spencer and Robert Shaw, were put in prison. There was no further playing until the autumn.

Meanwhile, Shakespeare had gained new notoriety. For some reason, which does not seem quite so obvious nowadays, the subjects of Queen Elizabeth in the 1590s found certain parallels between the political situation in the reign of Richard II and in their own times. It was never safe to make direct comment on current affairs, but historical plays and books which seemed to offer oblique political criticism were usually popular. Somehow it was felt that Queen Elizabeth resembled Richard II, and many of the followers of the Earl of Essex, who was now beginning to fall out of favour, saw in him a second Bolingbroke. In August 1597 Andrew Wise printed Shakespeare's *Richard II*. It was a most popular publication, and in six months went into three editions. The text, however, was incomplete, for the Deposition Scene was left out.

About this time, Shakespeare began to write the sequel to *Richard II* in the first part of *Henry IV*, which was another stage in the story of the curse on the House of Lancaster. Naturally, any story about Henry introduced his madcap son Prince Hal, who was a popular and legendary hero, and he had already appeared on the stage in an old play called *The Famous Victories of Henry V*, where his companion in mischief was called Sir John Oldcastle. When Shakespeare wrote the play in the autumn of 1597, London was swarming with captains who had returned with Essex from the expedition known as the Islands Voyage.* One of these Shakespeare began to envisage as Prince Hal's companion. He called him Sir John Oldcastle. This caused trouble. The real Sir John Oldcastle was burnt for his Lollard principles and seditious practices during the reign of Henry V, and therefore secured his place in *Foxe's Book of Martyrs*. Oldcastle was known also as Lord Cobham, and the Lord Cobham of Shakespeare's day, an unpleasant young man who had just succeeded to the title, objected. Shakespeare was obliged, therefore, to alter the name of Oldcastle, who henceforward became Falstaff.

In this play, too, he parodied one of his own most effective scenes. In this passage (ii, 4), where the Prodigal Prince rehearses

* See p. 101.

his interview with his father, Shakespeare made Falstaff play the stage King 'in Cambyses' vein' – an obvious and broad parody of the style and acting of Edward Alleyn. The parody was successful. Shakespeare followed the first part of *Henry IV* with a second part, into which he introduced a new character, Ancient Pistol, who stalked about the stage, strutting and behaving in Alleyn's manner with a vocabulary which was largely composed of ranting misquotations from plays in the repertory of the Admiral's Men.

The year 1598 was exciting in many ways for the Lord Chamberlain's Company. Falstaff from the very first was a great success. Then in the early autumn the Company put on a play by a new author who was beginning to make his name. Ben Jonson, after his imprisonment over the *Isle of Dogs* affair, joined the Lord Admiral's Men and was writing plays for them; but for some reason he parted from the Admiral's Men, with the result that his first good play, *Every Man in His Humour*, was offered to the Chamberlain's Men. They acted it in September with considerable success. The play had a sensational advertisement. Gabriel Spencer, who had been Jonson's companion in misfortune over the *Isle of Dogs*, waited for Jonson as he was coming from the playhouse and quarrelled with him. The two men fought each other in Hoxton Fields, and Spencer was killed. Jonson was again put in prison, but he was able to plead benefit of clergy and after a short time was released.

Matters with Giles Alleyn were now coming to a head. The lease of the Theatre ground had long expired and still nothing was settled. For the last few months the Company had left the Theatre and were playing in the Curtain. It was now clear that Alleyn meant to take advantage of the clause in the original lease and unless something drastic was done the Burbages would lose their valuable property.

The chief sharers in the Company, Richard Burbage and his brother Cuthbert, Shakespeare, John Heminges, Augustine Phillips, Thomas Pope, and Will Kempe, agreed to finance a new

21 Bankside, from Visscher's *View of London*, 1616

playhouse. By this new arrangement the Burbages held two-and-a-half shares and the others one apiece. In addition, as playing members of the Company, each held an actor's share of the takings. A new site was found on the Bankside not far from the Rose Theatre, and the lease was signed on 25 December 1598.

Three days later the two Burbages and a number of their friends, all armed, together with Peter Street, a builder who was to build the new playhouse, appeared outside the Theatre and proceeded to tear it down. The Theatre was a timber building and easily demolished. Giles Alleyn himself was away from London, but his people dared not interfere. The timber was then carried across the Thames and dumped on the new site. Meanwhile, until the new house was ready, the Company were still playing at the Curtain, where, early in April 1599, *Henry V* was produced.

The new playhouse – now the finest in London – was ready about July: it was called the Globe. By this time the Chamberlain's Men had a fine repertory, and their latest plays included

The Gally fuste

The Globe

22 The exterior of the Globe Playhouse: a detail from Plate 21

the two parts of *Henry IV* and *Henry V* and Jonson's *Every Man in His Humour*. To these were soon added Jonson's *Every Man out of His Humour*, Shakespeare's *As You Like It*, and *Julius Caesar*.

The competition with the Admiral's Men now became acute. Even while the Chamberlain's Men were separated by the river and the City, there had been bitter rivalry, but now that the two companies were playing side by side the Admiral's Men soon felt the effects. Accordingly, in October, they set their dramatists to work to provide a counter-attraction. This was a new and more or less historic version of the story of Sir John Oldcastle.

The play was put on for the first time on 1 November, and Henslowe, to show his appreciation, awarded the playwrights ten shillings as a gift. It was, however, soon obvious that the competition of the Chamberlain's Men would be too much for the Admiral's, and Alleyn decided to build a new theatre north of the river in the parish of St Giles. There were many vexatious delays, but ultimately, late in 1600, the new playhouse called the Fortune was finished and opened.

In the autumn of 1599 both Admiral's and Chamberlain's Men began to suffer from a new rival. William Stanley, Earl of Derby, was an enthusiastic amateur of plays. In November, at considerable cost, he revived the company of the Children of Paul's. The children of the choir of St Paul's Cathedral had not attempted to produce plays for the last nine years, but now the Earl of Derby set them going again, and John Marston, a young barrister who had recently distinguished himself as a virulent satirist, was brought in to provide them with plays. This investment was a success. As James Burbage had foreseen three years before, there was a great opening for a small private playhouse which would cater solely for gentlemen.

Others were interested. Henry Evans, a lawyer, who had been Lyly's partner in the former Boys' Company, saw a chance of starting a second company of Boys. He went into partnership with the Master of the Chapel Royal, Nathaniel Giles. Giles, by authority of his office, was empowered to impress likely boys into the Royal choir. Evans had his eye on the empty Blackfriars Theatre, which was a considerable burden to the Burbages, for they had to find the rent but could make no use of it. The objections to the presence of professional players in the Blackfriars neighbourhood did not apply so strongly to semi-private performances by choirboys. Evans therefore rented the Blackfriars playhouse from the Burbages on 2 September 1600, and in a very short time he had established another Children's Company, which was immediately prosperous.

Soon Ben Jonson, who seldom stayed long with one company, joined the Children of Blackfriars to provide plays for them. Marston offended Jonson by producing in his play *Histriomastix* a character called Chrysoganus – a close, though flattering, imitation of Jonson's Macilente in *Every Man out of His Humour*. Jonson took umbrage. He attacked Marston in his next play by making unpleasant hits at his person and his style. Marston countered, and for the next year a regular war of the Theatres was waged between the two Boy Companies.*

Early in 1601 the Chamberlain's Men were again in trouble. The fortunes of the Earl of Essex were now at their lowest; and he and his followers were planning a revolution. As part of their propaganda, some of Essex's friends approached the Company and asked them to act *Richard II*. The players were reluctant. The play had not been acted for some time and they did not believe that it would prove a good draw, but when Essex's friends promised to augment the takings with 40s. they agreed. Accordingly *Richard II* was acted on 7 February 1601. The next day was Essex's futile rising. When the Privy Council began to make inquiries the players were closely questioned about the affair, which was regarded as very sinister, but no action was taken and their indiscretion was overlooked.

Meanwhile the bickerings of the Children of Paul's and the Blackfriars were exciting genteel audiences. Both the professional Companies – Admiral's and Chamberlain's – felt the loss of their best customers. At last Ben Jonson, who was tiring of the struggle, decided to produce a play which would finally extinguish Marston. *Poetaster*, as the play was called, came out in

* For a short history of this affair, see my *Elizabethan Plays and Players*.

the autumn of 1601. It was put on by the Children of Black-friars.

The Chamberlain's Men and the Paul's united to retaliate. They hired Thomas Dekker, who had hitherto written for the Admiral's, to compose an answer to Ben Jonson. His play was called *Satiromastix* and followed *Poetaster* very shortly. Dekker was so much more skilful at abuse that Ben Jonson retired from play-writing for a couple of years. Shakespeare himself seems to have taken some part in this controversy. In the Christmas holidays the undergraduates of St John's College, Cambridge, acted a college play called *The Return from Parnassus*. They impersonated Burbage and Kempe who were brought in to give a lesson in acting, and they made Kempe say, 'O that Ben Jonson's a pestilent fellow; he brought up Horace giving the poets a pill, but our fellow Shakespeare has given him a purge that made him bewray his credit.' This play or scene has apparently disappeared.

During these months Shakespeare wrote *Hamlet*, in its present form, which was full of references to the events of the time.* About the same time he also wrote *Twelfth Night*, which was performed in the Hall of the Middle Temple on 2 February 1602.

In March 1603 Queen Elizabeth fell ill. As there was considerable doubt about the succession in the minds of the people at large, there was great alarm. On 19 March the Privy Council, who of late years had become increasingly suspicious of the theatre, ordered all playing to cease. Five days later, Queen Elizabeth died.

The death of the Queen actually advanced the fortunes of the players, and especially of the Chamberlain's Men. One of the first acts of the new King was to take the Company under his own protection. On 19 May they became the King's Men, and a licence (see p. 65) was granted to them. There was, however, little playing that summer, for once again the plague broke out in the City of London and continued for nearly a year. The

* For details see *Hamlet* in the Penguin Shakespeare.

players, as usual, were obliged to go on tour, but at Christmas-time they received a summons to come down to Wilton near Salisbury and there to play before the King and his Court. For this they received £30, for their expenses and for acting one play. By Christmas the plague was abating and the Court was held at Hampton Court. The Company acted six times in the Christmas holidays before the Court.

About this time Shakespeare wrote *Measure for Measure*, a sombre comedy in a new vein. In the autumn and winter of 1604–5 the players were much in request. On 1 November they played *Othello* in the Banqueting House at Whitehall; on the 4th, *The Merry Wives of Windsor*; on 26 December the *Comedy of Errors*; early in January *Love's Labour's Lost* and *Henry V*. On 10 February they played *The Merchant of Venice*, which so pleased King James that he ordered it to be played again on the 12th.

Shakespeare was now apparently writing less for the Company, but in 1606 and again in 1607 he wrote at least three plays. *Lear* and *Macbeth* were probably written in 1606, and *Antony and Cleopatra* in 1607–8.

There were many changes and developments during these years. The Boys' Companies flourished for some years and attracted to themselves some of the best writers of the time. Chapman was writing regularly for them; and in 1607 began the famous partnership of Francis Beaumont and John Fletcher, who wrote *Philaster* and *The Maid's Tragedy* for the Blackfriars Children.

In 1608, however, the Children of Blackfriars were abruptly turned out of their playhouse. From the first they were a nuisance to the authorities. The temptation to appeal to their small audiences by constantly commenting on current affairs was too great. In 1605 they produced *Eastward Ho*, a play written by Jonson, Marston, and Chapman, in which they even had the impudence to deride the Scots who were swarming about the Court in London, and to mimic King James's Scots accent; it d considerable trouble. In 1608 they offended unforgivably. Chapman wrote a play called *The Conspiracy and Tragedy of Charles, Duke of Byron*, which dealt with the rebellion and death of the Duke in Paris in 1602. It was recent history, and concerned living persons. Chapman even brought on the stage the reigning French King, Henry IV, together with his Queen and his mistress. In one scene the Queen was shown boxing the ears of her rival. The French Ambassador protested, and the Boys were forbidden to act the play. A few days later, when the Court left London, they disobeyed this order. As a result the Company was for a time dissolved. Evans and his partners in the Blackfriars were now left with an empty playhouse on their hands, and they asked the Burbages to release them from their agreement.

The King's Men welcomed the chance. Conditions had changed considerably in the last eleven years, and there was no longer any serious opposition to the players occupying the Blackfriars playhouse. Moreover, the Globe Theatre was found to have its drawbacks. It was built on marshy ground, which in winter became very muddy. Accordingly, in August 1608, Richard Burbage joined in partnership with his brother Cuthbert, Shakespeare, Heminges, Condell, and Sly, and his former tenant Evans. They took over the private playhouse for winter use, and, in addition, they purchased the plays belonging to the Children and agreed to employ their dramatists.

The different conditions in the private playhouses are reflected in the plays produced in the years following. The Globe Theatre was open to the air and plays were acted by daylight. In the Blackfriars Theatre plays were acted by candlelight. Far more elaborate and subtle stage effects were therefore possible. Moreover, as the players now mainly concerned themselves with a better-class audience, drama tended to become more sophisticated and less public.

Shakespeare appears to have written little between 1608 and 1610 when the theatres were again closed for many months because of plague, though the epidemic was far less serious than in 1592–3 or 1603. Then in 1610 and 1611 he wrote his last three comedies, *Cymbeline*, *The Winter's Tale*, and *The Tempest*. *The Tempest* was acted for the King on 1 November 1611, and *The Winter's Tale* on 5 November. Shakespeare, however, seems now to have spent most of his time at Stratford. On 2 July 1613, his career as a dramatist was symbolically ended in the destruction of the Globe Theatre when the players were acting *Henry VIII* with considerable magnificence. The disaster caused much comment, and there are a number of references to it. The most detailed is in a letter written by Sir Henry Wotton:

Now, to let matter of State sleep, I will entertain you at the present with what has happened this week at the Bankside. The King's Players had a new play, called *All is True*, representing some principal pieces of the reign of Henry VIII, which was set forth with many extraordinary circumstances of pomp and majesty, even to the matting of the stage, the Knights of the Order with their Georges and Garters, the Guards with their embroidered coats, and the like: sufficient in truth within a while to make greatness very familiar, if not ridiculous. Now, King Henry making a masque at the Cardinal Wolsey's house, and certain cannons being shot off at his entry, some of the paper, or other stuff, wherewith one of them was stopped, did light on the thatch, where being thought at first but an idle smoke, and their eyes more attentive to the show, it kindled inwardly, and ran round like a train, consuming within less than an hour the whole house to the very ground.

This was the fatal period of that virtuous fabric, wherein yet nothing did perish, but wood and straw, and a few forsaken cloaks; only one man had his breeches set on fire, that would perhaps have broiled him, if he had not by the benefit of a provident wit put it out with bottle-ale.

It is possible that the disaster was greater than Wotton realized, for it may be that some of Shakespeare's plays perished in the fire.

6

Shakespeare's Theatre

Drama, of all forms of art, is most immediately affected by material circumstance. The poet or the novelist can wait for recognition, perhaps for years, but a dramatist, and especially one who is also a sharer in the playhouse and company which produces his plays, cannot afford a failure. He must please his public or he will go bankrupt. He appeals, not to future ages, but to the audience of the afternoon. His plays therefore must be written to suit the stage on which they will be performed, the company which is to act them, and the audience which will pay to see them.

Until James Burbage built the Theatre in 1576, Elizabethan players had no permanent home. They were accustomed to act on a variety of stages. They gave private performances in the great halls of noblemen's houses or in one of the Queen's palaces, or the Inns of Court, and they acted in public in Town Halls and inn yards, or in any place where they could erect a stage and collect a crowd.

The stage used by travelling players was simple – a platform of boards resting on trestles or barrels, with a curtained booth at the back where the actors could change their costumes or wait for the cue for entrance. The evolution from this kind of stage to the elaboration of the Fortune has been well traced in a series of reconstructions by C. Walter Hodges in *The Globe Restored*, 1953, some of whose drawings are here reproduced. The notes at the foot of each are by Mr Hodges.

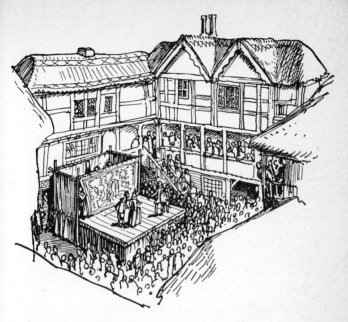

23 Stage in an inn yard, *c.* 1565

The stage shown here is based upon two pictures, one from the
sixteenth century by Pieter Balten, and the other from the
seventeenth by Callot. The stages they show are almost identical.
The sketch above is intended to represent a provincial fit-up. In the
more firmly established conditions obtaining for a while at the great
London inns this arrangement may have been modified somewhat,
the stage perhaps being married up with the surrounding buildings,
but the general effect was probably much the same.

Unfortunately the Elizabethan Age is very inadequately illustrated. Many interesting details of life in town and country in the
fourteenth and fifteenth centuries are preserved in the miniatures
of illustrated manuscripts; and from 1550 to 1650 life in the Low
Countries is vividly illustrated in the paintings of Peter Breughel

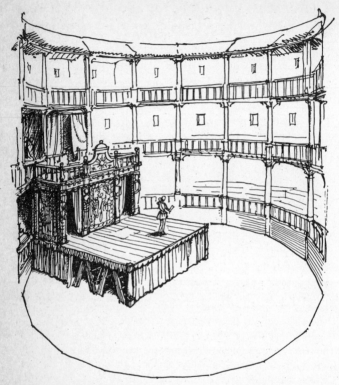

24 Stage in an amphitheatre, *c.* 1576

The little stage and booth has now been moved into an arena, but it can be dismounted and removed if the yard is wanted for the 'game of bulls and bears'. When the stage is in position the galleries adjoining it are taken over as back-stage area. The top of the booth has here been boarded over and railed in, so that it can be used as an acting place, and it is rather more elaborately decorated than formerly.

and his successors. There is nothing comparable by English artists. Most of the woodcuts and engravings in books are crude and amateur, and few artists painted good landscapes. Nor did any English artist leave a picture of the inside of an Elizabethan theatre.

Modern reconstructions of the Elizabethan stage are thus largely guesswork, based upon such evidence as survives. This evidence is of three kinds: (*a*) the Swan drawing; (*b*) stage directions in early texts and casual references in books and letters; and (*c*) the contracts for building the Fortune Theatre in 1600 and the Hope in 1612 – both in the *Henslowe Papers*.

25 A playhouse, *c*. 1595

This sketch is based upon the Swan drawing. The top-storey opening within the Heavens is conjectural. The position of the Heavens hut, set fairly low within the encircling roof, is in accordance with several authentic views. The main weight of the hut is here carried upon the line of the tiring-house façade.

26 The Fortune Theatre, 1600

The overall dimensions and layout are according to the contract, but details are necessarily conjectural. I here assume that the building was set with the tiring-house backing on to the street, and that the audience entered the yard along the gangways on either side of the stage. 'Iron pikes', as in the contract, are placed along the parapet of the bottom gallery to prevent persons climbing over from the yard. Upper galleries are reached by stairs in the angles of the building near the street.

(a) *The Swan drawing.* Only one contemporary sketch of the Elizabethan stage survives. A Dutchman named ·Johannes de Witt visited London about 1596 and made a sketch of the stage of the Swan Theatre. The sketch was copied by his friend Arend von Buchel (see Pl. 28). The draughtsmanship is crude, and its accuracy cannot be tested. Nor does it follow that even if the sketch is accurate, other stages were built on the same pattern.

(b) *Stage directions.* In the early Elizabethan texts stage directions are erratic and usually lack the fuller details of setting and action provided by modern dramatists. From time to time, however, they reveal details of the stage business which show something of the necessary equipment of the stage. One of the more interesting texts is *Coriolanus* as printed in the First Folio. Among its stage directions are the following:

Enter a Company of Mutinous Citizens, with Staues, Clubs, and other weapons.

Enter Volumnia and Virgilia, mother and wife to Martius: They set them downe on two lowe stooles and sowe.

Enter Martius, Titus Lartius, with Drumme and Colours, with Captaines and Souldiers, as before the City Corialus: to them a Messenger.

They Sound a Parley: Enter two Senators with others on the Walles of Corialus.

Another Alarum, and Martius followes them to the gates, and is shut in.

Flourish. Alarum. A Retreate is sounded. Enter at one Doore Cominius with the Romanes: At another Doore Martius, with his Arme in a sling.

Enter two officers, to lay cushions, as it were, in the Capitoll.

A Sennet. Enter the Patricians, and the Tribunes of the People, Lictors before them; Coriolanus, Menenius, Cominius and the Consul: Sicinius and Brutus take their places by themselues: Coriolanus stands.

Enter two Senators, with Ladies, passing ouer the Stage with other Lords.

These directions require a stage which was provided with two doors (at least); a set of gates; and an upper stage representing the walls of 'Corialus'. For the meeting of the Senate, benches, stools, or chairs are needed; these could have been carried in or already set behind a curtain which would be drawn aside at the proper moment. There is, however, little in the play which could not have been presented on the stage of the Swan drawing. Moreover, as those who argue for the accuracy of the drawing point out, that stage is very similar to the acting space available in great halls where the players often performed.

Many great halls survive and are still in use. In the colleges at Oxford and Cambridge, the Halls of the Inns of Court in London, Hampton Court, and elsewhere. They are all of a pattern. At one end is the dais where the more illustrious sit; at the other the 'screen' through which are two doors leading to the kitchen beneath the 'minstrels'' gallery. With this screen as background,

The Globe Playhouse 1599–1613

27 A Conjectural Reconstruction
   by C. Walter Hodges

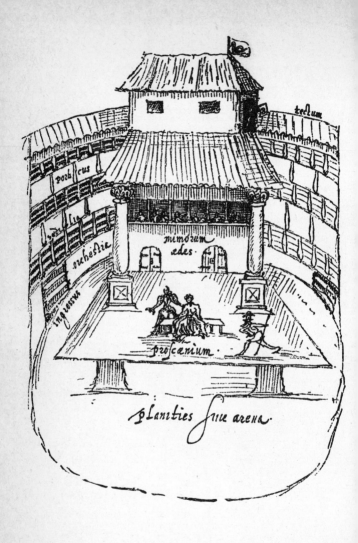

28 The Swan Theatre: the drawing by Johannes de Witt about 1596

the players acted, using both doors and gallery as part of their stage (see Pl. 29).

(c) *The Fortune contract.* In 1600, Henslowe and Alleyn, disturbed by the competition from the new Globe playhouse, decided to build a new theatre, on the opposite side of the City of London, to be named the Fortune. They called in Peter Street, the builder of the Globe, and a detailed and elaborate contract was drawn up, which is so important a document of stage history that it is worth reprinting in full:

THIS INDENTURE made the eighth day of January, 1599 [1600], and in the two and fortieth year of the reign of our sovereign Lady Elizabeth, by the grace of God Queen of England, France and Ireland, defender of the faith, &c, Between Phillip Henslowe and Edward Alleyn of the parish of Saint Saviours in Southwark, in the county of Surrey, gentlemen, on the one part, And Peter Street, citizen and carpenter of London, on the other part, WITNESSETH that, whereas the said Phillip Henslowe and Edward Alleyn the day of the date hereof have bargained, compounded and agreed with the said Peter Street for the erecting, building, and setting up of a new house and stage for a playhouse, in and upon a certain plot or parcel of ground appointed out for that purpose, situate and being near Golding Lane in the parish of Saint Giles without Cripplegate of London To be by him the said Peter Street, or some other sufficient workmen of his providing and appointment, and at his proper costs and charges, for the consideration hereafter in these presents expressed, made, erected, builded and set up, in manner and form following; that is to say,

The frame of the said house to be set square, and to contain fourscore foot of lawful assize every way square without, and fifty-five foot of like assize square every way within, with a good, sure, and strong foundation of piles, brick, lime, and sand, both without and within, to be wrought one foot of assize at the least above the ground.

And the said frame to contain three stories in height. The first or lower story to contain twelve foot of lawful assize in height, the second story eleven foot of lawful assize in height, And the third or upper story to contain nine foot of lawful assize in height.

All which stories shall contain twelve foot and a half of lawful assize in breadth throughout, besides a jutty forwards in either of the said two upper stories of ten inches of lawful assize, with four convenient divisions for gentlemen's rooms, and other sufficient and convenient divisions for twopenny rooms, with necessary seats to be placed and set as well in those rooms as throughout all the rest of the galleries of the said house; and with such like stairs, conveyances, and divisions, without and within, as are made and contrived in and to the late erected playhouse on the Bank, in the said parish of Saint Saviours, called the Globe;

With a Stage and Tiring-house to be made, erected and set up within the said frame, with a shadow or cover over the said stage, which stage shall be placed and set, as also the staircases of the said frame, in such sort as is prefigured in a plot thereof drawn,

And which stage shall contain in length forty and three foot of lawful assize, and in breadth to extend to the middle of the yard of the said house.

The same stage to be paled in below with good strong and sufficient new oaken boards.

And likewise the lower story of the said frame withinside, and the same lower story to be also laid over and fenced with strong iron pikes,

And the said stage to be in all other proportions contrived and fashioned like unto the stage of the said playhouse called the Globe; with convenient windows and lights glazed to the said tiring-house.

And the said frame, stage and staircases to be covered with tile, and to have a sufficient gutter of lead, to carry and convey the water from the covering of the said stage to fall backwards,

And also all the said frame and the staircases thereof to be sufficiently enclosed without with lath, lime and hair, and the gentlemen's rooms and twopenny rooms to be sealed with lath, lime and hair; and all the floors of the said galleries, stories and stage to be boarded with good and sufficient new deal boards of the whole thickness, where need shall be.

And the said house, and other things before mentioned to be made and done, to be in all other contrivitions, conveyances, fashions, thing and things, effected, finished, and done according to the manner and fashion of the said house called the Globe.

29 Middle Temple Hall

Saving only that all the principal and main posts of the said frame and stage forward, shall be square and wrought pilasterwise, with carved proportions called Satyrs to be placed and set on top of every of the same posts.

And saving also that the said Peter Street shall not be charged with any manner of painting in or about the said frame, house, or stage, or any part thereof, nor rendering the walls within nor ceiling any more or other rooms than the gentlemen's rooms, twopenny rooms and stage, before remembered.

Now THEREUPON the said Peter Street doth covenant, promise and grant for himself, his executors and administrators, to and with the said Phillip Henslowe and Edward Alleyn, and either of them and the executors and administrators of them, and either of them by these presents, in manner and form following, that is to say,

That he the said Peter Street, his executors or assigns, shall and will, at his or their own proper costs and charges, well, workmanlike and substantially make, erect, set up and fully finish in and by all things, according to the true meaning of these presents, with good, strong, and substantial new timber and other necessary stuff,

All the said frame and other works whatsoever in and upon the said plot or parcel of ground (being not by any authority restrained, and having ingress, egress and regress to do the same) before the five and twentieth day of July next coming after the date hereof;

AND SHALL ALSO at his or their like costs and charges, provide and find all manner of workmen, timber, joists, rafters, boards, doors, bolts, hinges, brick, tile, lath, lime, hair, sand, nails, lead, iron, glass, workmanship and other things whatsoever, which shall be needful, convenient and necessary for the said frame and works and every part thereof,

AND shall also make all the said frame in every point for scantlings larger and bigger in assize than the scantlings of the timber of the said new erected house called the Globe.

AND ALSO that he the said Peter Street shall forthwith, as well by himself as by such other and so many workmen as shall be convenient and necessary, enter into and upon the said buildings and works,

30 The Great Hall of Hampton Court Palace

And shall in reasonable manner proceed therein, without any wilful detraction until the same shall be fully effected and finished.

IN CONSIDERATION of all which buildings, and of all stuff and workmanship hereto belonging,

The said Phillip Henslowe and Edward Alleyn, and either of them, for themselves, their and either of their executors and administrators, do jointly and severally covenant to grant to and with the said Peter Street, his executors and administrators, by these presents,

That they the said Phillip Henslowe and Edward Alleyn, or one of them or the executors, administrators or assigns of them or one of them, shall and will well and truly pay or cause to be paid unto the said Peter Street, his executors or assigns, at the place aforesaid appointed for the erecting of the said frame, The full sum of four hundred and forty pounds of lawful money of England, in manner and form following, that is to say, At such time And when as the timber work of the said frame shall be raised and set up by the said Peter Street, his executors or assigns or within seven days then next following, two hundred and twenty pounds,

And at such time and when as the said frame and work shall be fully effected and finished as is aforesaid, or within seven days then next following, the other two hundred and twenty pounds, without fraud or covin.

PROVIDED ALWAYS, and it is agreed between the said parties, That whatsoever sum or sums of money the said Phillip Henslowe and Edward Alleyn, or either of them, or the executors or assigns of them or either of them shall lend or deliver unto the said Peter Street, his executors or assigns or any other by his appointment or consent, for or concerning the said works or any part thereof, or any stuff thereto belonging, before the raising and setting up of the said frame, shall be reputed, accepted, taken and accounted in part of the first payment aforesaid of the said sum of four hundred and forty pounds;

And all such sum and sums of money as they, or any of them, shall as aforesaid lend or deliver between the raising of the said frame and

---

31 The Globe Theatre: a wood-engraving by R.J.Beedham after a reconstruction by Dr J.C.Adams

finishing thereof, and of all the rest of the said works, shall be reputed, accepted, taken and accounted in part of the last payment aforesaid of the same sum of four hundred and forty pounds; anything above said to the contrary not withstanding.

IN WITNESS WHEREOF the parties above said to these present indentures interchangeably have set their hands and seals. Given the day and year first above-written.*

As the contract shows, the Elizabethan playhouse was small. The external dimensions were only 80 by 80 feet; and of the interior area of 55 by 55 feet, left between the galleries, the stage occupied almost half. Even by modern standards, the size of the stage is considerable. Unfortunately the contract is vague about the stage itself; all details are 'prefigured in a plot (or plan) thereof drawn' – and the plot has perished. The contract says nothing about doors, or upper stage; nor does it mention the size or the location of the 'tiring-house'. A tiring-house was the place where the actors changed their attire, and presumably it was at the rear of the stage; but there is endless controversy about its size, arrangement, and relation to the rest of the acting area.

One notable attempt to reconstruct the stage and its appearance is shown in J. C. Adams' model (Pl. 31). Adams claimed that the whole back section from roof to floor was the tiring area; that behind the stage proper there was an inner stage, concealed by a curtain when not in use, of the same depth as the galleries (which he called the Study); an upper stage also concealed by a curtain (which he called the Chamber); an upmost area normally used by musicians but available on occasion for a lookout or the like.

If the stage was so divided, then Shakespeare could have used considerable variety in locating his scenes, different areas denoting different sets of characters. Thus, in the First Act of *Antony and Cleopatra* the main action would be presented on the stage proper, but the scenes which concern Cleopatra and her women (I, iii; I, v; II, v; III, iii) could be shown in the room above. Such a

* *Henslowe Papers*, edited by W. W. Greg, p. 4.

method of shifting the action from main stage to upper stage, and, at times, to inner stage, is quite effective when used in modern productions played in theatres of the Elizabethan kind. There is, unfortunately, no certain evidence to show whether Shakespeare was aware of these possibilities.

Many of Adams' views have been rejected by later scholars, mainly on the ground that there is not enough evidence for his reconstruction and that it is contrary to the Swan drawing which shows a blank space between the two doors, and no trace of any inner stage. Nevertheless an acting place, which can be revealed by drawing a curtain at the rear of the main stage, is clearly demanded for several plays: for Juliet's tomb, for the discovery of the statue of Hermione in *The Winter's Tale*, for the discovery of Ferdinand and Miranda playing chess in *The Tempest*, for a hiding place for Claudius and Polonius in *Hamlet* III, i. For such incidents some suggest that a temporary booth was erected on the main stage as on the inn-yard scaffold (see Pl. 23). However, a permanent inner stage, whether full-size as in Adams' model, or a mere recess, is far more convenient and so more likely.

This inner stage was used not only for discoveries, but also for concealments. One major problem, often overlooked by recent writers on Elizabethan stagecraft, is the staging of the final moments of those tragedies which end with several corpses lying on the stage. Unless the corpse got up and walked away, only two methods are possible: either the body was carried off, or else it was concealed within a recess; for the Elizabethan stage had no general stage curtain.

The single corpse was no problem. It was solemnly borne out and the funeral procession made a fitting end. Thus in *Julius Caesar*, Brutus has committed suicide. Octavius says:

> According to his virtue, let us use him
> With all respect, and rites of burial.
> Within my tent his bones tonight shall lie,
> Most like a soldier ordered honourably:

> So call the field to rest, and let's away,
> To part the glories of this happy day.
> *Exeunt omnes*

In *Coriolanus* the end is quite elaborately detailed. Aufidius, having killed Coriolanus, suffers a reaction:

> My rage is gone,
> And I am struck with sorrow. Take him up:
> Help three a' th' chiefest soldiers, I'll be one.
> Beat thou the drum that it speak mournfully:
> Trail your steel pikes. Though in this City he
> Hath widow'd and unchilded many a one,
> Which to this hour bewail the injury,
> Yet he shall have a noble memory. Assist.
> *Exeunt, bearing the body of Martius.*
> *A dead March sounded.*

In *Romeo and Juliet* and in *Othello* there was another kind of problem; two corpses are lying on a bier or bed and one on the floor. In both plays the dead were concealed by drawing a curtain; and for this action in each play there is a cue in the dialogue. In *Romeo and Juliet*, the Prince comments:

> Seal up the mouth of outrage for a while,
> Till we can clear these ambiguities.

And in *Othello*, Lodovico says:

> The object poisons sight,
> Let it be hid.

It follows that the suicide and dying speeches of Romeo and of Juliet, and the strangling of Desdemona and the suicide of Othello were played at the back of the stage in an area deep and wide enough for a bed which was finally hidden by drawing a curtain; and that some of Shakespeare's plays were written for a stage which was provided with an inner stage of some kind, though it is not possible to be sure of its nature, size, or shape. On the whole Adams' solution seems more probable than others.

A combination of both methods – procession and concealment – is indicated for the end of *Hamlet* and of *Lear*. In *Hamlet*, the dead are Hamlet, Claudius, Gertrude, and Laertes. By Fortinbras's command Hamlet is carried off ceremoniously:

> Let four captains
> Bear Hamlet like a soldier to the stage,
> For he was likely, had he been put on
> To have prov'd most royally: and for his passage,
> The soldiers' music, and the rites of war
> Speak loudly for him.
> Take up the body;* such a sight as this
> Becomes the field, but here shows much amiss.
> Go, bid the soldiers shoot.
> > *Exeunt marching: after the which a peal of ordnance*
> > *are shot off.*

Hamlet is thus given a four-bearer funeral, which means five actors. How were the other three corpses removed? If carried out in procession, each would require a minimum of two bearers apiece even if everyone lent a hand, including Fortinbras, Horatio, and Osric. This calls for at least fourteen actors. More likely, the King and Gertrude fell within the inner area where either Laertes also fell or was carried. The curtain was then closed to allow full attention to be concentrated on the funeral of Hamlet. There is a similar situation at the end of *Lear* where there are five corpses – Lear, Cordelia, Edmund, Goneril, and Regan.

Such are some of the problems to be considered in any reconstruction of the Elizabethan stage.

In the Fortune contract the playhouse was to be square, but the few pictures that remain of the outside of other theatres show that they were circular or octagonal (see, e.g. Pl. 22). Within the outer walls there were three tiers of galleries, looking down on the stage and the yard where the poorer spectators stood. The

* This is the Folio reading; the Second Quarto reads 'bodies', which is less likely to have been correct.

stage itself, technically known as an 'apron stage', jutted out into the yard, so that when the house was full the players were surrounded on three sides. Over the stage the 'shadow' or roof protected the players from the rain.

The structure of the stage considerably affected the form of Elizabethan plays. In the modern theatre the actor is separated from his audience by a curtain which conceals or reveals the whole stage. Moreover, he acts in bright light before spectators hidden in a darkened auditorium. On the apron stage the actor came forward in daylight into the midst of his audience. He and they were thus, as it were, fused into a common experience. The device of soliloquy was not, as on the modern stage, embarrassingly artificial, but a quite natural communication as a character explains his thoughts and intentions to those immediately before him. As there was no need for him to shout, the greatest subtlety of voice, gesture, and expression was possible. Nor needed he to speak slowly; in that small auditorium every word could easily be heard, and the spectators were eager and trained listeners.

Apparently there was no scenery apart from an occasional property gate, tree, or the like, and plays were acted in daylight. The Elizabethan actor was thus without the lighting, scenery, sound effects, and other realistic or symbolic adjuncts of the modern stage. In their place he gained his effects by a direct assault on the emotions and the imagination of the spectators. Poetry was thus a natural medium for dramatic speech, especially at exalted moments, and a good actor could carry his audience with him by the emotional force of rhetoric.

The action was continuous. A scene ended when all the actors had gone off the stage and a new set of characters came on. There was thus a quick continuity of performance with no break in the illusion. As there was no scenery, so there was no limit to the number of scenes. Usually the exact locality of the scene was unimportant. When it was necessary Shakespeare showed it in the dialogue.

'What country, friends, is this?' Viola asks.

'This is Illyria, lady,' the sea captain answers.

But for the most part a simple property or garment was sufficient. Chairs or stools showed indoor scenes; a man wearing riding-boots was a messenger; a king wearing his armour was on the field of battle; a watchman carrying a lantern indicated the streets of a city at night. The most important difference between the modern and the Elizabethan theatre is that on the public stages there was no curtain to divide the stage from the auditorium.

Such arrangements are simple, but not crude. All drama implies an acceptance of conventions and a use of the imagination, and properties can easily replace scenery. The properties were many and varied. Amongst the *Henslowe Papers* is a complete inventory of the properties belonging to the Admiral's Company in 1598:

i rock, i cage, i tomb, i Hell mouth.

i tomb of Guido, i tomb of Dido, i bedstead.

viii lances, i pair of stairs for Phaeton.

ii steeples, & i chime of bells, & i beacon.

i heifer for the play of Phaeton, the limbs dead.

i globe, & i golden sceptre; iii clubs.

ii marchpanes, & the City of Rome.

i golden fleece; ii rackets; i bay tree.

i wooden hatchet; i leather hatchet.

i wooden canopy; old Mahomet's head.

i lion skin; i bear's skin; & Phaeton's limbs & Phaeton's chariot; & Argus' head.

Neptune's fork and garland.

i 'croser's' staff; Kent's wooden leg.

Iris head, & rainbow; i little altar.

viii vizards; Tamberlain's bridle; i wooden mattock.

Cupid's bow, & quiver; the cloth of the Sun & Moon.

i boar's head & Cerberus' iii heads.

i Caduceus; ii moss banks, & i snake.

ii fans of feathers; Bellendon stable; i tree of golden apples; Tantalus' tree, ix iron targets.

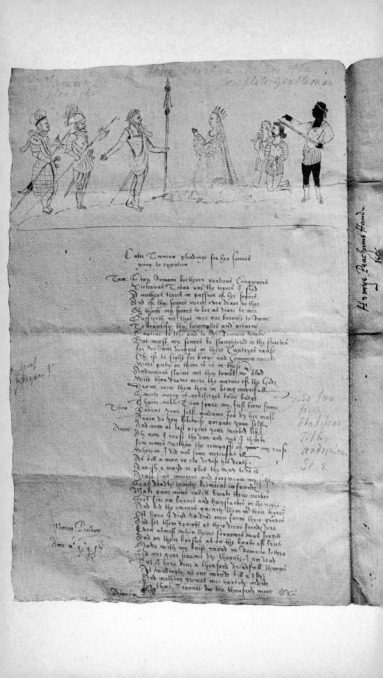

H: Peacham Hand
1616

Enter Tamora pleadinge for her sonnes
goyng to execution

Tam: Stay Romane bretheren gratious Conquerour
Victorious Titus rue the teares I shed
A mothers teares in passion for her sonnes
And if thy sonnes were ever deare to thee
Oh thinke my sonnes to bee as deare to mee
Suffiseth not that wee are browght to Roome
To beautifye thy triumphes and returne
Captiue to thee and to thy Romane yoake
But must my sonnes be slaughtered in the streetes
for valiant dooynges in there Cuntryes cause
Oh if to fight for kinge and Common weale
Weare piety in thine it is in these
Andronicus staine not thy tombe wth blod
Wilt thou drawe neere the nature off the Gods
Drawe neere them then in beinge mercifull
Sweete mercy is nobilityes true badg
Thryce noble Titus spare my first borne sonne

Titus: Patient your selfe madame for by her must
Raxon do you likewise prepare your selfe
And now at last repent your wicked life

Aron: Ah now I curse the day and yet I thinke
few comes within the compasse off my curse
wherein I did not some notorious ill
As kill a man or els deuise his death
Rauish a mayd or plott the way to do it
Accuse some innocent and forsweare my selfe
Set deadly enmity betweene two freinds
Make poore mens cattell breake there necks
Set fire on barnes and haystackes in the night
And bid the owners quench them wth there teares
Oft haue I digd vp dead men from there graues
And set them vpright at there deere freinds dore
euen almost when theire sorrowes was forgott
And on there breastes as on the barke off tr[ees]
Haue with my knife carued in Romane letters
Let not your sorrow dye thowgh I am dead
Tut I haue done a thowsand dreadfull thinges
As willingly as one would kill a fly
And nothing greiues mee hartily indeede
But that I cannot do ten thowsand more

Henry Peacham
Anno m͞o gq͞q͞q͞q

So far
then
Stabber
Titus
Andronicus
Sc. 2

i copper target, & xvii foils.

iiii wooden targets; i greeve armour.

i sign for Mother Redcap; i buckler.

Mercury's wings; Tasso's picture; i helmet with a dragon; i shield, with
   iii lions; i elm bowl.

i chain of dragons; i gilt spear.

ii coffins; i bull's head; and i 'vylter'.

iii timbrels; i dragon in Faustus.

i lion; ii lion's heads; i great horse with his legs; i sackbut.

i wheel and frame in the Siege of London.

i pair of wrought gloves.

i Pope's mitre.

iii Imperial crowns; i plain crown.

i ghost's crown; i crown with a sun.

i frame for the heading in Black Joan.

i black dog.

i cauldron for the Jew.*

[This list is reproduced in modern spelling. Henslowe's spelling was
erratic and individual, and some of the interpretations are questionable.
It is not known how 'Hell mouth' or the 'City of Rome' were represented as properties. Of the others, a 'marchpane' was an elaborate
marzipan cake; the 'frame for the heading' was a piece of stage
machinery to produce the illusion of a beheading.]

There was some attempt at realistic presentation. When
characters were stabbed they bled, as Caesar is made to bleed in
Julius Caesar. In the play of *Arden of Feversham* there was a fog,
which must have been represented somehow. The stage machinery
was, however, crude and irritating to the artistic sense of Ben
Jonson, who sneered at it in the prologue to the revised version
of *Every Man in His Humour*:

> He rather prays you will be pleased to see
> One such to-day, as other plays should be;

* *Henslowe Papers*, p. 116.

32 A production of *Titus Andronicus*, c. 1594: the first illustration to
Shakespeare. Drawing probably by Henry Peacham. Longleat

> Where neither Chorus wafts you o'er the seas,
> Nor creaking throne comes down the boys to please;
> Nor nimble squib is seen to make afeard
> The gentlewomen; nor rolled bullet heard
> To say, it thunders; nor tempestuous drum
> Rumbles, to tell you when the storm doth come.

On the other hand costumes were sometimes lavish and imposing. When in 1601 the Admiral's Men produced a play of Cardinal Wolsey they bought 'two pile velvet of carnadine at twenty shillings a yard, satins at twelve shillings and taffetas at twelve and six'. The bill for material alone came to £21 in money of the day. An inventory of costumes in the *Henslowe Papers*, probably of the same date as the inventory of properties, lists eighty-four garments of various kinds, most of them magnificent, such as 'a short velvet cloak embroidered with gold and gold spangles', 'a crimson robe striped with gold, faced with ermine', 'a cardinal's gown'.

There seems to have been little attempt at historical accuracy; the Romans in *Julius Caesar* and *Coriolanus* wore doublets, cloaks, and large hats; Cleopatra was tight-laced in a 'busk'. In *Troilus and Cressida*, Hector and Ajax fought by the rules of medieval combat and in *Lear* (nominally a prehistoric play) Edgar wore a closed helmet which covered his face. On the other hand, when portraying recent events the players sometimes took special care over the costuming. In January 1597 English troops under Sir Francis Vere and Sir Robert Sidney greatly distinguished themselves at the battle of Turnhout in Brabant. In October 1599 the battle was dramatized, probably by Shakespeare's Company, with characters named after the originals, and the actor portraying Vere was made up with a beard resembling his and wearing a watchet satin doublet with hose trimmed with silver.*

Again, in 1601 Charles, Duke of Biron (who held in France much the same position as had Essex in England) paid a state visit to Queen Elizabeth with a large band of followers, all of

* *Elizabethan Journals*, 24 October 1599.

whom wore black. Hereupon Sir Walter Ralegh spent all night with his tailor and next day appeared in Court with a black taffeta suit and a black saddle on his horse. A year later – July 1602 – Biron was executed in the Bastille for high treason. This event, coming so soon after Essex's fall and Biron's visit, caused a great sensation. Within three months, Worcester's players were acting a play of the life and death of Biron, for which on 25 September Henslowe laid out £5 to 'bye a blacke sewt of satten', and 14s. to make a scaffold and bar.*

Only one contemporary picture remains of a performance of a Shakespearean play – a sketch made by Henry Peacham in 1595 of an incident in the opening scene of *Titus Andronicus* where Tamora Queen of Goths pleads with Titus for her two sons (see Pl. 32). In the picture, Titus, Aaron the Moor, and the two sons wear 'renaissance-classical' military garb, Tamora wears flowing draperies, while the two soldiers supporting Titus are in more or less contemporary Elizabethan costume. Such a mixture of styles is likely enough, though it is as well not to place too much reliance on this picture, which may be as unreliable for evidence of costume as the old posters which used to advertise pre-cinema melodramas – attractively lurid in themselves but having small resemblance to anything that would be seen in the actual production.

There was an elaborate system of trumpet calls; sennets, tuckets, alarums, retreats, flourishes, appear frequently in stage directions. No king enters or goes out without a flourish. On the modern stage these trumpet calls are usually half-hearted: on the Elizabethan they had a considerable psychological effect. The stage directions, especially of some of Greene's plays produced at the Rose Theatre, show that the stage carpenter was ambitious:

Let there be a brazen head set in the middle of the place behind the Stage, out of which cast flames of fire, drums rumble within: Enter two Priests.

* *Elizabethan Journals*, 14 September 1601; *Henslowe's Diary*, i, 181, 182.

Exit Venus; or if you conveniently can, let a chair come down from the top of the stage and draw her up.

The Magi with their rods beat the ground, and from under the same riseth a brave arbour; the King returneth in another suit, while the Trumpets sound.

Upon this prayer she departeth, and a flame of fire appeareth from beneath, and Radagon is swallowed.

Jonas the Prophet cast out of the Whale's belly upon the stage.

Henslowe's record of the daily takings shows that plays at the Rose Theatre were acted on the repertory system. The Company kept a considerable range of plays available and played a different play each afternoon. The average life of a new play was about ten performances. Popular plays were acted more often, but the less successful sometimes disappeared after the second or third performance. Continuous runs were unknown. In a typical period of four weeks – February 1596 – the Admiral's Men played the following plays:

2nd *The Jew of Malta*	16th *The Blind Beggar*
3rd *First part of Fortunatus*	17th *The Jew of Malta*
4th *The Wise Man of Westchester*	18th *Olympio*
5th *Longshanks*	19th *The Blind Beggar*
6th *Harry the Fifth*	20th *Fortunatus*
7th *Crack me This Nut*	22nd *The Blind Beggar*
9th *Pythagoras*	23rd *Pythagoras*
10th *Fortunatus*	24th *Chinon*
11th *Chinon of England*	25th *Seven Days of the Week*
12th *The Blind Beggar of Alexandria*	26th *The Blind Beggar*
13th *Dr Faustus*	27th *Longshanks*
15th *Pythagoras*	

Thus on twenty-three acting days, eleven different plays were acted. Of these one – *The Blind Beggar of Alexandria* – was new and successful; it was played five times during the month. Of the remaining ten, seven no longer survive. A large proportion of Elizabethan plays have perished.

It follows that the Elizabethan actor was a busy man, constantly rehearsing new plays. He had little time for long, elaborate, and exhausting preparations; but he belonged to a team and the trained actor was ready in emergency to improvise, and Italian actors at this time were so clever that, given a story, they could make up the play as they went along.

The Elizabethan acting Company was a permanent 'fellowship of players', and they worked on the share system. Since the actors were partners in the concern, the Company remained constant. There were ten to fifteen regular sharers, and in addition some hired men and boys learning the business who ultimately might rise to be sharers.

Amongst Henslowe's *Papers* there is an agreement between Henslowe and Jacob Meade with an actor named Robert Dawes. Dawes agrees for a space of three years to play with such Company as Phillip Henslowe and Jacob Meade shall agree:

at the rate of one whole share according to the custom of the players; and that he the said Robert Dawes shall and will at all times during the said term duly attend all such rehearsal which shall the night before the rehearsal be given publicly out; and if that he the said Robert Dawes shall at any time fail to come at the hour appointed, then he shall and will pay to the said Phillip Henslowe and Jacob Meade their executors or assigns twelve pence; and that if he come not before the said rehearsal is ended then the said Robert Dawes is contented to pay two shillings; and further that if the said Robert Dawes shall not every day whereon any play is or ought to be played be ready apparelled and . . . to begin the play at the hour of three of the clock in the afternoon unless by six of the same Company he shall be licensed to the contrary, that then he the said Robert Dawes shall and will pay unto the said Phillip and Jacob or their assigns three shillings, and that if that he the said Robert Dawes happen to be overcome with drink at the time when he ought to play, by the judgement of four of the said company, he shall and will pay ten shillings and if he the said Robert Dawes shall·fail to come during any play having no license or just excuse of sickness he is contented to pay twenty shillings.

The agreement then proceeds to discuss the problem of wearing-apparel and adds the clause that if Dawes

shall at any time after the play is ended depart or go out of the house with any of their apparel on his body or if the said Robert Dawes shall carry away any property belonging to the said company, or shall be consenting or privy to any other of the said company going out of the house with any of their apparel on his or their bodies, he the said Robert Dawes shall and will forfeit and pay unto the said Phillip and Jacob or their administrators or assigns the sum of forty pounds of lawful money of England.*

The importance of the Company system is considerable. Nowadays a director assembles actors suitable for a particular play, and he can draw from a vast reservoir of all kinds and types. If he needs an actor who specializes in taking the part of a chimpanzee, he will find several available. Shakespeare had to write for his Company as it existed. He could not therefore produce characters for which the Company had no physical representative. On the other hand he made use of the peculiarities of the actors, and it is noticeable how certain physical types recur. In the Company there was a tall man with a thin hatchet face. In *2 Henry IV* he is Shadow – a 'half-faced fellow'; and probably he doubled the part of the beadle who hustles Doll Tearsheet to prison, a 'thin man in a censer'; 'a starved bloodhound', 'goodman death, goodman bones'. He was Sir Andrew Aguecheek in *Twelfth Night*, who was as tall as any man in Illyria, but when Toby was less restrained, 'a cockscomb and a knave, a thin faced knave'. He was Slender in *The Merry Wives*, 'a latten bilbo' and 'a little wee face'. And since he was clearly a success in gull or silly gentlemen parts, he was probably also Monsieur Le Beau in *As You Like It*, Master Matthew in Jonson's *Every Man in His Humour*, Fastidious Brisk in *Every Man out of His Humour*,

* *Henslowe Papers*, p. 123.

33 Richard Burbage: perhaps a self-portrait. A detail from the picture in the Dulwich Gallery

Asinius Bubo in Dekker's *Satiromastix*, Osric in *Hamlet*, and Roderigo in *Othello*.

The two star actors in the Company were Richard Burbage and William Kempe. Burbage's great reputation dates from the foundation of the Chamberlain's Men in 1594. The parts he is recorded as having taken are Lear, Hamlet, Brachiano in Webster's *The White Devil*, Malevole in Marston's comedy *The Malcontent*, and, most famous of all, Richard in *Richard III*. Richard was an early success and Burbage's cry of 'A horse, a horse, my Kingdom for a horse' was the most often quoted and parodied of all Shakespeare's lines.

Will Kempe the new Company's Clown was a very different kind of actor. He was older than Burbage and Shakespeare and was already famous when he joined the Company in 1594, having made a great reputation in England and on the continent as a low comedian and a dancer of jigs, mostly indecent. He is known to have taken the parts of Peter the Nurse's man in *Romeo and Juliet*, and Dogberry in *Much Ado*. Kempe remained with the Chamberlain's Men for six or seven years, but in 1600, during the season of Lent when playing was prohibited, he made bets that he would dance from London to Norwich. He completed the journey in nine stages; and when he reached Norwich four weeks after his start, he was given a civic welcome by the Mayor. Encouraged by this success, Kempe became more ambitious, and in 1601 he undertook to dance over the Alps to Rome; but the journey was a failure and he was back in London in September. He did not rejoin the Chamberlain's Company.

Kempe seems to have been an ignorant man who relied for laughs on his clowning, grimaces, and extempore wit. The rest of the Company were glad to see him go, nor did they welcome his return to London in the autumn of 1601 when he joined Worcester's Men then playing at the Rose, next door to the Globe. It is probably with Kempe in mind that Hamlet rebukes the ambitious Clown:

And let those that play your Clowns, speak no more than is set down for them. For there be of them, that will themselves laugh, to set on some quantity of barren spectators to laugh too, though in the mean time, some necessary question of the play be then to be considered: that's villainous, and shows a most pitiful ambition in the Fool that uses it.

In the pirated first Quarto of *Hamlet* there is an additional passage:

And then you have some again that keep one suit of jests, as a man is known by one suit of apparel, and gentlemen quote his jests down in their tables before they come to the play, as thus: 'Cannot you stay till I eat my porridge?' and 'You owe me a quarter's wages,' and 'My coat wants a cullison,' and 'Your beer is sour,' and blabbering with his lips, and thus keeping in his cinquepace of jests, when God knows the warm clown cannot make a jest unless by chance, as the blind man catcheth a hare. Masters tell him of it.

Kempe was followed by Robert Armin, a very different kind of comedian. While Kempe was a Clown, Armin was rather a Singing Fool, witty, sophisticated, and pathetic. For him Shakespeare wrote the parts of Touchstone, Feste, and Lear's Fool.

In Shakespeare's time there were no women actresses. The parts of young women were acted by boys. This was not necessarily a great disadvantage; since a boy could only act a girl's part till his voice broke, Shakespeare was spared Rosalinds and Violas of forty-five. Moreover the boys must have been quite competent; for many of the plays depend on the ability and charm of the women, especially the three romantic comedies of *Much Ado*, *As You Like It*, and *Twelfth Night*. In these plays one of the women was small: Hero is 'too low for a high praise, too brown for a fair praise, and too little for a great praise'; Celia is 'low and browner than her brother' (i.e., Ganymede alias Rosalind); Maria is the little villain, the 'youngest wren of nine'. From about 1605 to 1608 the Company evidently included a boy who was remarkable for his portrayal of emotional and wicked women;

for him Shakespeare wrote the parts of Lady Macbeth, Goneril, and Cleopatra. In 1610, he was succeeded by another boy who was charming as an adolescent girl in such parts as Marina, Imogen, Perdita, and Miranda.

The Chamberlain's Men seems to have been a close-knit fellowship, and the friendship of the chief members was lifelong. When Shakespeare died – more than twenty years after the Company was first formed – he left memorial rings to 'my fellows John Heminges, Richard Burbage, and Henry Condell'. Seven months later Burbage named his new-born infant William; and – most important of all – seven years later Heminges and Condell saw the First Folio through the press.

7

The Shakespeare Canon

In any study of the development of Shakespeare's art the date
when each play was written must first be discovered. This is not
so easy. So few of the necessary records survive that Elizabethan
plays can seldom be exactly dated. Plays acted by the companies
which played in Henslowe's theatres are recorded in his diary,
which gives either the date of the first performance, or else details
of the payments made to dramatists. But only a small proportion
of the plays written during Shakespeare's lifetime were acted at
the Rose or Fortune playhouses; for the other companies and
playhouses there is no record comparable to the *Diary*.

Shakespeare's plays must therefore be dated by argument, and
deduction from such evidence as can be collected. This is of
three kinds: (*a*) *external*; (*b*) *internal*; (*c*) *style*. By combining
all kinds of evidence the canon of the plays has been worked out,
and there is general agreement on the approximate dates at which
most of the plays were written.

(*a*) The most valuable kind of evidence is external, that is, a
clear mention or reference to a particular play. There are many
of these references. Thus in *Gesta Grayorum*, an account of the
famous 'Gray's Inn Revels' of 1594–5, there is a note that:

on the night of the 28th December, 1594, after dancing and revelling
with gentlewomen, a 'Comedy of Errors' (like to Plautus his 'Menech-
mus') was played by the players.

A German traveller named Platter who came to London in 1599 noted in his diary a visit to the Globe Theatre:

> After dinner on the 21st of September, at about two o'clock, I went with my companions over the water, and in the strewn roof-house [i.e. playhouse with thatched roof] saw the tragedy of the first Emperor Julius with at least fifteen characters very well acted. At the end of the comedy they danced according to their custom with extreme elegance. Two in men's clothes and two in women's gave this performance, in wonderful combination with each other.*

Simon Forman, a notorious astrologer and quack who had dealings with many fashionable women about the Court of James I, made notes of some plays which he watched in the spring of 1611, including *Macbeth*, *Cymbeline*, and *The Winter's Tale*. Of *Macbeth* he wrote:

> In Mackbeth at the Glob, 1610 [1611], the 20 of Aprill [Saturday], ther was to be obserued, firste, howe Mackbeth and Bancko, 2 noble men of Scotland, Ridinge thorowe a wod, the[r] stode before them 3 women feiries or Nimphes, And saluted Mackbeth, sayinge, 3 tyms vnto him, haille Mackbeth, king of Codon; for thou shalt be a kinge, but shalt beget No kinges, &c. Then said Bancko, What all to Mackbeth And nothing to me. Yes, said the nimphes, haille to thee Bancko, thou shalt beget kinges, yet be no kinge. And so they departed & cam to the Courte of Scotland to Dunkin king of Scotes, and yt was in the dais of Edward the Confessor. And Dunkin bad them both kindly well-come, And made Mackbeth forth with Prince of Northumberland, and sent him hom to his own castell, and appointed Mackbeth to prouid for him, for he would sup with him the next dai at night, & did soe. And Mackbeth contriued to kill Dunkin, & thorowe the persuasion of his wife did that night Murder the kinge in his own Castell, beinge his guest. And ther were many prodigies seen that night & the dai before. And when Mack Beth had murdred the kinge, the blod on his handes could not be washed of by Any meanes, nor from his wiues handes, which handled the bloddi daggers in hiding them, By which means they became both moch amazed & Affronted. The murder being knowen,

---

* E. K. Chambers, *The Elizabethan Stage*, ii, 364–5.

Dunkins 2 sonns fled, the one to England, the [other to] Walles, to saue them selues, they being fled, they supposed guilty of the murder of their father, which was nothinge so. Then was Mackbeth crowned kinge, and then he for feare of Banko, his old companion, that he should beget kinges but be no kinge him selfe, he contriued the death of Banko and caused him to be Murdred on the way as he Rode. The next night, beinge at supper with his noble men whom he had bid to a feaste to the which also Banco should haue com, he began to speake of Noble Banco, and to wish that he wer ther. And as he thus did, standing vp to drincke a Carouse to him, the ghoste of Banco came and sate down in his cheier behind him. And he turninge About to sit down Again sawe the goste of Banco, which fronted him so, that he fell into a great pas-sion of fear and fury, Vtterynge many wordes about his murder, by which, when they hard that Banco was Murdred they Suspected Mackbet.

Then MackDove fled to England to the kinges sonn, And soe they Raised an Army, And cam into Scotland, and at Dunston Anyse over-thrue Mackbet. In the meantyme whille Macdouee was in England, Mackbet slewe Mackdoues wife & Children, and after in the battelle Mackdoue slewe Mackbet.

Obserue Also howe Mackbetes quen did Rise in the night in her slepe, & walke and talked and confessed all & the doctor noted her wordes.*

The 'Revels Accounts' of the Court show that payments were made in 1604-5 for a performance of *Othello* before King James I and his Court on 1 November, on 4 November for *The Merry Wives of Windsor*, and 26 December for *Measure for Measure*; in January for *Love's Labour's Lost*, on 7 January for *Henry V*, and on 10 February for *The Merchant of Venice*, repeated on the 12th. Later, payments were made for *The Tempest*, acted before the King on 1 November 1611, and again in February 1613, at the marriage festivities of the Princess Elizabeth.

Valuable evidence for the dates of the earlier plays is given in

* E. K. Chambers, *William Shakespeare*, ii, 337–8. The original spelling has been kept.

Francis Meres' list of a dozen quoted on pp. 13–14. These plays at least were produced before Meres' book went to press in the summer of 1598. Moreover it is probable that other plays, more important, had not then been produced, otherwise Meres would hardly have failed to mention *Twelfth Night*, *Hamlet*, *Othello*, and *Lear*.

External evidence seldom gives the date of the first performance of any play, but it certainly shows that the play had been written before a certain date.

(*b*) The second kind of evidence is internal, where in the play itself there is some unmistakable reference to an identifiable event. There are not many of these in Shakespeare's plays, for although he often reminded his audience of current events in some significant speech, he seldom made a direct reference.

There is, however, a clear reference to the triumphant departure, on 27 March 1599, of the Earl of Essex for Ireland in the *Chorus* before Act v of *Henry V*:

> But now behold,
> In the quick forge and working-house of thought,
> How London doth pour out her citizens,
> The Mayor and all his brethren in best sort,
> Like to the Senators of th'antique Rome,
> With the plebeians swarming at their heels,
> Go forth and fetch their conquering Caesar in:
> As by a lower, but by loving likelihood,
> Were now the General of our gracious Empress,
> As in good time he may, from Ireland coming,
> Bringing rebellion broached on his sword;
> How many would the peaceful City quit,
> To welcome him?

As Essex failed utterly and returned secretly to London on 28 September, it follows that the *Chorus* was written soon after March and some time before September 1599.

In *Hamlet* there is a reference to the war of the theatres in 1600–1 (see p. 115) in Hamlet's remarks:

HAMLET: What players are they?

ROSENCRANTZ: Even those you were wont to take delight in, the tragedians of the City.

HAMLET: How chances it they travel? their residence both in reputation and profit was better both ways.

ROSENCRANTZ: I think their inhibition comes by the means of the late innovation.

HAMLET: Do they hold the same estimation they did when I was in the City? are they so follow'd?

ROSENCRANTZ: No indeed, they are not.

HAMLET: How comes it? do they grow rusty?

ROSENCRANTZ: Nay, their endeavour keeps in the wonted pace; but there is sir an aery of children, little eyases, that cry out on the top of question; and are most tyrannically clapp'd for't: these are now the fashion, and so berattle the common Stages (so they call them) that many wearing rapiers, are afraid of goose-quills, and dare scarce come thither.

HAMLET: What, are they children? who maintains 'em? how are they escoted? Will they pursue the quality no longer than they can sing? will they not say afterwards if they should grow themselves to common Players (as it is most like if their means are no better) their writers do them wrong, to make them exclaim against their own succession?

ROSENCRANTZ: Faith there has been much to do on both sides: and the nation holds it no sin, to tarre them to controversy. There was for a while, no money bid for argument, unless the Poet and the Player went to cuffs in the question.

HAMLET: Is't possible?

GUILDENSTERN: O there has been much throwing about of brains.

HAMLET: Do the Boys carry it away?

ROSENCRANTZ: Ay that they do my Lord, Hercules and his load too.

Sometimes the internal evidence in a play consists of several casual topicalities, none very significant or certain in themselves, but taken together fairly conclusive. Thus, *As You Like It* can be dated with some probability as 'summer 1599'. The latest date is fixed by a note in the Stationers' Register (dated 4 August 1600) that *As You Like It*, *Henry the Fifth*, *Every Man in His Humour*, and the Comedy of *Much Ado about Nothing* are to be 'stayed', that is, not printed until the printer has established his right to print.

In the play itself there is a quotation from Marlowe's *Hero and Leander*:

> Dead Shepherd, now I find thy saw of might:
> Whoever loved that loved not at first sight.   (III, v, 81)

Hero and Leander was left unfinished at Marlowe's death on 30 May 1593; it was first printed in 1598.

There are other topicalities. Celia remarks, 'Since the little wit that fools have was silenced, the little foolery that wise men have makes a great show' (I, ii, 94). In June 1599 the Privy Council ordered that eight of the more scurrilous books of satires should be called in and burnt.

Jaques' famous speech on the Seven Ages of Man begins:

> All the world's a stage,
> And all the men and women, merely Players.

As it happened, in the early summer of 1599 the Chamberlain's Men had just moved into their new theatre – the Globe – which bore as its motto *Totus mundus agit histrionem* – 'all the world plays the player'.

The evidence for the date of *Twelfth Night* is even fuller. The latest date is fixed by an entry dated 2 February 1602, in the diary of John Manningham, a barrister of the Middle Temple:

At our feast we had a play called 'Twelfth Night, or What you Will,' much like the Comedy of Errors, or Menechmi in Plautus, but most like and near to that in Italian called *Inganni*. A good practice in it to make the Steward believe his Lady widow was in love with him, by counterfeiting a letter as from his Lady in general terms, telling him what she liked best in him, and prescribing his gesture in smiling, his apparel, etc., and then when he came to practise making believe they took him to be mad.

This was likely to have been, if not the first, at least an early performance, for the young lawyers of the Inns of Court were keen playgoers to whom the players would offer their newest rather than an older play.

The date is supported by various topicalities in the text itself. Maria says of Malvolio that 'he does smile his face into more lines, than is in the new map, with the augmentation of the Indies' (III, ii, 84). This map appeared in 1600, and was the first English map drawn on the principle of Mercator's projection; it was remarkable for the many rhumb lines indicating comparative distances.

Again, Fabian says, 'I will not give my part of this sport for a pension of thousands to be paid from the Sophy' (II, v, 196). Persia was being much talked about. In 1597 Sir Anthony Shirley set out with his brother Robert and a party of Englishmen on a mission to the Sophy (Shah) of Persia. After many adventures on the way, they were kindly treated and well rewarded. Some of the party returned to London, by way of Russia, in September 1600; but Shirley was much suspected as he had been a hot partisan of Essex. An account of the voyage was immediately printed but in October 1600 it was suppressed by order of the Council and all copies burnt. A year later – 11 November 1601 – a longer account was entered for printing in the Stationers' Register. As he borrowed a few phrases from this book for *Hamlet*, Shakespeare evidently read it.

In III, i, 67 Viola comments on the Fool:

> This fellow is wise enough to play the fool,
> And to do that well, craves a kind of wit:
> He must observe their mood on whom he jests,
> The quality of persons, and the time:
> And like the haggard, check at every feather
> That comes before his eye. This is a practice,

> As full of labour as a wise man's art:
> For folly that he wisely shows, is fit;
> But wise men folly-fall'n, quite taint their wit.

Robert Armin, who succeeded Kempe as the Company's Clown in 1600, was expert at composing verses extempore. Some time in 1600 or early in 1601 he printed a collection of these trifles in a volume called *Quips upon Questions*. One of his topics was 'He plays the Fool' of which the first two of five stanzas run:

> True it is, he plays the fool indeed,
> But in the play, he plays it as he must;
> Yet when the play is ended, then his speed
> Is better than the pleasures of thy trust.
>> For he shall have what thou that time has spent,
>> Playing the fool, thy folly to content.
>
> He plays the wise man then, and not the fool
> That wisely for his living can do so.
> So doth the carpenter with his sharp tool,
> Cut his own finger oft, yet lives by't too.
>> He is a fool to cut his limb, say I,
>> But not so with his tool to live thereby.

To this poem he added a 'Quip':

> A merry man is often thought unwise,
> Yet mirth in modesty's loved of the wise.
> Then say, should he for a fool go
> When he's a more fool that accounts him so?
> Many men descant on another's wit
> When they have less themselves in doing it.

Shakespeare at greater leisure rewrote this effort of the Company's new Clown.

In describing the wreck, the Captain (I, ii, 10) says:

> When you, and those poor number saved with you,
> Hung on our driving boat: I saw your brother
> Most provident in peril, bind himself,

(Courage and hope both teaching him the practice)
To a strong mast, that liv'd upon the sea.

A pamphlet called *News from Ostend*, entered 5 August 1601, described the escape in a sea fight of a man who

committed himself to the mercy of God and the merciless seas upon a piece of a mast rather than that he would fall into the hands of his bloody enemies. After he had so floated upon the waves of the sea an hour or two he was taken up by another ship which had spied the man driving on the water.*

The name of the melancholy Duke – Orsino – Shakespeare took from a real person. In the winter of 1600–1 Virginio Orsino, Duke of Bracciano, visited England and was entertained at Court, where Shakespeare's Company played before him, but there is no record of the plays acted. It is unlikely that Shakespeare would have risked trouble by giving the same name to a character in the play as was borne by so distinguished a spectator. A year later there would have been no risk.

Lear can also be closely dated. The latest possible date of writing is fixed by the title page of the quarto of 1608 (see p. 215) which states that the play was acted at Court on 26 December 1606. By this time the King's Men had performed before the King at least thirty-three times; a Christmas play was therefore likely to have been new. The earliest possible date of writing was 1603. Edgar disguised as Poor Tom the Bedlam beggar says:

. . . . five fiends have been in poor Tom at once; of lust, as Obidicut, Hobbididance Prince of dumbness, Mahu of stealing, Modo of murder, Flibbertigibbet of mopping and mowing who since possesses chambermaids and waiting-women. (IV, i, 63)

These names Shakespeare took from a book called *A Declaration of Egregious Popish Impostures* which was written by the Rev. Samuel Harsnett, Chaplain to the Bishop of London, and published early in 1603.

* *Last Elizabethan Journal*, 25 July 1601.

It is possible to get nearer. In the play, Gloucester, who was a believer in omens and portents, says to Edmund:

These late eclipses in the sun and moon portend no good to us: though the wisdom of Nature can reason it thus, and thus, yet Nature finds itself scourg'd by the sequent effects. Love cools, friendship falls off, brothers divide. In cities, mutinies; in countries, discord; in palaces, treason; and the bond crack'd, 'twixt son and father. This villain of mine comes under the prediction; there's son against father; the King falls from bias of Nature, there's father against child. We have seen the best of our time. Machinations, hollowness, treachery, and all ruinous disorders follow us disquietly to our graves. (ɪ, ii, 112)

A little later Edmund, speaking to Edgar, cynically echoes Gloucester's words:

I am thinking, brother, of a prediction I read this other day, what should follow these eclipses . . . I promise you, the effects he writes of, succeed unhappily, as of unnaturalness between the child and the parent, death, dearth, dissolutions of ancient amities, divisions in state, menaces and maledictions against King and nobles, needless diffidences, banishment of friends, dissipation of cohorts, nuptial breaches, and I know not what. (ɪ, ii, 152)

Shakespeare took these speeches from a little pamphlet called *Strange, fearful and true news which happened at Carlstadt in the Kingdom of Croatia*. The events were certainly strange and fearful. The sun shone red like blood for nine successive days. Two armies were seen in the air fighting. A woman gave birth to three sons, of which one had four heads that uttered strange things. The pamphlet was translated from the High Dutch. These terrible signs, according to the editor, one Edward Gresham an almanack maker, were divine portents of threatening disaster:

The Earth's and Moon's late and horrible obscurations, the frequent eclipsations of the fixed bodies; by the wandering, the fixed stars, I mean the planets, within these few years more than ordinary, shall without doubt (salved divine inhibition) have their effects no less admirable, than the positions unusual. Which PEUCER with many more too long to rehearse out of continual observation and the consent of all authors noted to be, new leagues, traitorous designments, catching at kingdoms, translation of empire, downfall of men in authority, emulations, ambition, innovations, factious sects, schisms and much disturbance and troubles in religion and matters of the Church, with many other things infallible in sequent such orbical positions and phenomenes.

The preface to *Strange News from Croatia* was dated 11 February 1606. The similarity of sentiment, phrase, and rhythm between the passages in the play and the pamphlet can hardly be accidental.

On March 1606 a storm of wind of exceptional violence, the worst in living memory, caused vast damage not only in England but all over Northern Europe, blowing down churches, and almost overwhelming the town of Flushing. It may be that this storm inspired Shakespeare to drive Lear out into the storm so vividly described in Act III and also to write the description of the storm which followed the murder of Duncan in *Macbeth*. There were no storms in the sources from which *Lear* and *Macbeth* were taken.

The description of Dover Cliff (IV, vi, 11) would also seem to have been based on actual observation. Shakespeare's Company visited Dover in September 1606.

When Lear has gone mad he observes sagely to the Bedlam beggar (III, iv, 159):

> First let me talk with this philosopher,
> What is the cause of thunder?

A remark which would have raised a laugh at the Court performance, for everyone had recently been talking about the cause of thunder. In November the church at Bletchingley in Surrey was struck by lightning and consumed by fire, and the bells were melted into fragments. The event was much talked of, as is shown in a book written soon after by the Rev. Simon Harward called *A Discourse of Lightning* in which he discussed the various explanations of the disaster, particularly the sins of the townsmen (which he denied to be worse than others). He then considered at length the opinions of philosophers and astronomers concerning the natural causes of thunder and lightning.

All in all the evidence suggests that *Lear* was begun in the spring of 1606 and finished late in the year.

(*c*) The third method of dating, by style, is most difficult, for there are no reliable objective tests which can be mechanically applied. Nevertheless the changes and developments in Shakespeare's style are so noticeable that a play can reasonably be placed by style alone in one of four groups – *Early*, *Mature*, *Concentrated*, and *Late*. But style needs separate treatment.

By a combination of the three methods most plays can be dated approximately and placed roughly in the order of their writing, so that it is possible not only to trace Shakespeare's development but also to see his plays against the background of his times.

The full list of Shakespeare's works is as follows:

Approximate Date	Plays	First Printed
By 1594	HENRY VI (*three parts*)	*Folio* 1623
	THE TWO GENTLEMEN OF VERONA	*Folio*
	THE COMEDY OF ERRORS	*Folio*
	THE TAMING OF THE SHREW	*Folio*
	RICHARD III	1597
	TITUS ANDRONICUS	1594
	LOVE'S LABOUR'S LOST	1598
1594–1597	ROMEO AND JULIET (*pirated* 1597)	1599
	A MIDSUMMER NIGHT'S DREAM	1600
	RICHARD II	1597
	KING JOHN	*Folio*
	THE MERCHANT OF VENICE	1600
1597–1600	HENRY IV (Part I)	1598
	HENRY IV (Part II)	1600
	HENRY V (*pirated* 1600)	*Folio*

	MUCH ADO ABOUT NOTHING	
	MERRY WIVES OF WINDSOR (*pirated* 1602)	
	AS YOU LIKE IT	*Folio*
	JULIUS CAESAR	*Folio*
	TROILUS AND CRESSIDA	1609
1601–1608	HAMLET (*pirated* 1603)	1604
	TWELFTH NIGHT	*Folio*
	MEASURE FOR MEASURE	*Folio*
	ALL'S WELL THAT ENDS WELL	*Folio*
	OTHELLO	1622
	LEAR	1608
	MACBETH	*Folio*
	TIMON OF ATHENS	*Folio*
	ANTONY AND CLEOPATRA	*Folio*
	CORIOLANUS	*Folio*
After 1608	PERICLES (*omitted from the Folio*)	1609
	CYMBELINE	*Folio*
	THE WINTER'S TALE	*Folio*
	THE TEMPEST	*Folio*
1613	HENRY VIII	*Folio*

Poems

VENUS AND ADONIS	1593
THE RAPE OF LUCRECE	1594
SONNETS A LOVER'S COMPLAINT }	1609
THE PHOENIX AND THE TURTLE	1601

The Development of Shakespeare's Style

When Shakespeare began to write for the stage the standard of acting was set by Edward Alleyn, and of plays by those who wrote for him, especially Marlowe, Greene, and Kyd. Alleyn's most popular plays were Marlowe's *Tamburlaine* and *Jew of Malta*, Greene's *Orlando Furioso* and *Friar Bacon*, and Kyd's *Spanish Tragedy*. All had much in common, and at first Shakespeare imitated the common style and mannerisms so closely that some critics argue hotly whether he was indeed the sole author of some of the early plays attributed to him in the First Folio.

Audiences in the early 1590s were still unsophisticated, simple in their demands, and hearty in their appetites. They expected characters on the stage to talk in high-sounding phrases and to make long speeches on every occasion, full of rhetorical devices, stuffed with mythology and bookish similes. Thus Marlowe, wishing to express the perplexities of Zenocrate, torn between affection for her father and her former love, and her new love for Tamburlaine, makes her say:

> Now shame and duty, love and fear presents
> A thousand sorrows to my martyred soul.
> Whom should I wish the fatal victory,
> When my poor pleasures are divided thus,
> And racked by duty from my cursed heart?
> My father and my first betrothed love
> Must fight against my life and present love;

Wherein the change I use condemns my faith,
And makes my deeds infamous through the world.
But as the gods, to end the Trojan's toil,
Prevented Turnus of Lavinia,
And fatally enriched Aeneas' love,
So, for a final issue to my griefs,
To pacify my country and my love,
Must Tamburlaine by their resistless powers,
With virtue of a gentle victory,
Conclude a league of honour to my hope;
Then, as the powers divine have pre-ordained,
With happy safety of my father's life
Send like defence of fair Arabia.

This is the language of the literary student who turns naturally to Virgil for an apt parallel in Turnus and Aeneas, pleasing to those who have also read the *Aeneid* but quite inappropriate to the distressed Egyptian damsel.

Marlowe was more successful in writing blank verse than the others, but even he could not keep a kind of shuttle rhythm out of his lines. He did not attempt to write blank verse as in any way representing normal speech: his aim was to be gorgeous and magnificent, to write in 'high astounding terms' which suited the style of Alleyn and his company, who liked sound and fury.

At first Shakespeare admired the current fashions. He revelled in mere words, their sound, colour, and glitter. He was at his best in comedy and he liked rhyme, for he often moved more freely within the restraints of rhyme than in the freer blank verse. Comedy was still his natural outlet. It gave him the chance of choosing words and phrases with an ease and subtlety which, though this kind of cleverness has long passed out of fashion, no one else ever touched. It is shown at its best in *Love's Labour's Lost* in such a speech as the defence of 'barbarism' which he gave to Berowne, a bubbling, many-coloured cascade of words. The thought is simple: that those who neglect everything for the sake of learning and never fall in love, miss more than they gain by their studies. In this speech he takes up the idea of light and darkness, to juggle with them in a dazzling display of verbal trickery:

> Why! all delights are vain, and that most vain
> Which with pain purchas'd, doth inherit pain,
> As painfully to pore upon a book,
> To seek the light of truth, while truth the while
> Doth falsely blind the eyesight of his look:
> Light seeking light, doth light of light beguile:
> So ere you find where light in darkness lies,
> Your light grows dark by losing of your eyes.
> Study me how to please the eye indeed,
> By fixing it upon a fairer eye,
> Who dazzling so, that eye shall be his heed,
> And give him light that it was blinded by.
> Study is like the heaven's glorious Sun,
> That will not be deep-search'd with saucy looks:
> Small have continual plodders ever won,
> Save base authority from others' books.
> These earthly godfathers of heaven's lights,
> That give a name to every fixed star,
> Have no more profit of their shining nights,
> Than those that walk and wot not what they are.
> Too much to know, is to know nought but fame:
> And every godfather can give a name.

The four-fold 'light', each with a slightly different meaning, in

> Light seeking light, doth light of light beguile,

is an amazingly clever trick.

The outburst is neither profound thought nor good drama, for everything must stand still until Berowne has finished. It is the sheer exuberance of an athlete who has discovered that he can play what game he likes with words. Yet the speech itself is significant. It is the answer of the 'upstart crow', whose Latin was little and Greek less, to those intellectual snobs who believed that all learning lived in books. Shakespeare's lack of book-learning was a blessing. When he needed a simile or an image he found it in his own experience and not in his reading.

In his early tragedies Shakespeare was less successful. He was still inclined to be heavy, especially when he wrote for effect. In *Richard III* Tyrrel describes the death of the little princes – an occasion for pathos and sentimentality:

> The tyrannous and bloody act is done,
> The most arch deed of piteous massacre
> That ever yet this Land was guilty of:
> Dighton and Forrest, who I did suborn
> To do this piece of ruthful butchery,
> Albeit they were fleshed villains, bloody dogs,
> Melting with tenderness, and mild compassion,
> Wept like to children, in their death's sad story.
> O thus (quoth Dighton) lay the gentle Babes:
> Thus, thus (quoth Forrest) girdling one another
> Within their alabaster innocent arms:
> Their lips were four red roses on a stalk,
> And in their summer beauty kissed each other.
> A Book of Prayers on their pillow lay,
> Which once (quoth Forrest) almost chang'd my mind:
> But O the Devil, there the villain stopped:
> When Dighton thus told on, we smothered
> The most replenished sweet work of Nature,
> That from the prime Creation ere she framed.
> Hence both are gone with conscience and remorse,
> They could not speak, and so I left them both,
> To bear this tidings to the bloody King.

There is a sense of strain in the passage. Lines are hammered out to fit the pattern of the metre –

> That éver yét this lánd was gúilty óf.

Even the image of lips 'like four red roses on a stalk' is pretty rather than apt, deliberately sentimental. The whole description is written for effect and without real feeling: it is painted passion.

Shakespeare's earliest style is quite distinguishable. His rhythms are regular; rhymes are common, used sometimes in alternate lines, more often in couplets. Occasionally he even inserts a sonnet into the dialogue. In the comedies there is much clever language, especially when young gentlemen are talking (which is sometimes tedious, for wit changes its fashion quickly), and an excessive outpouring of 'three-piled hyperboles'; imagery is often used for its own sake and not to clarify or intensify thought. In tragedy, and especially historical tragedy, Shakespeare was often bombastic and speeches were more heroic than suited the occasion. Shakespeare was still more interested in fine writing than in drama.

The best and the worst traits of his immature style are to be seen in the finest of his early plays, *Romeo and Juliet*. Lady Capulet urges Juliet to fall in love with Count Paris in a speech which for twelve lines plays with the far-fetched conceit that Paris is a book:

> Read o'er the volume of young Paris' face,
> And find delight, writ there with beauty's pen,
> Examine every married lineament,
> And see how one another lends content:
> And what obscur'd in this fair volume lies,
> Find written in the margent of his eyes.
> This precious book of love, this unbound lover,
> To beautify him, only lacks a cover:
> The fish lives in the sea, and 'tis much pride
> For fair without, the fair within to hide:
> That book in many's eyes doth share the glory
> That in gold clasps locks in the golden story:
> So shall you share all that he doth possess,
> By having him, making yourself no less.

This is tediously clever.

Later Juliet, impatiently waiting for night and Romeo, breaks out into a lyric ecstasy which is just as elaborately poetical, but yet perfect:

> Gallop apace, you fiery-footed steeds,
> Towards Phoebus' lodging, such a waggoner
> As Phaethon would whip you to the west,
> And bring in cloudy night immediately.
> Spread thy close curtain love-performing night,
> That runaways eyes may wink, and Romeo
> Leap to these arms, untalk'd of and unseen,
> Lovers can see to do their amorous rites,
> By their own beauties, or if love be blind,
> It best agrees with night: come civil night,
> Thou sober-suited matron all in black,
> And learn me how to lose a winning match,
> Play'd for a pair of stainless maidenhoods.
> Hood my unmann'd blood baiting in my cheeks,
> With thy black mantle, till strange love grow bold,
> Think true love acted simple modesty:
> Come night, come Romeo, come thou day in night,
> For thou wilt lie upon the wings of night,
> Whiter than new snow on a raven's back:
> Come gentle night, come loving black-brow'd night,
> Give me my Romeo, and when he shall die,
> Take him and cut him out in little stars,
> And he will make the face of heaven so fine,
> That all the world will be in love with night,
> And pay no worship to garish Sun.
> O I have bought the mansion of a love,
> But not possess'd it, and though I am sold,
> Not yet enjoy'd, so tedious is this day,
> As is the night before some festival,
> To an impatient child that hath new robes
> And may not wear them.

The early style disappeared rapidly as Shakespeare's experiences grew and with them his power of expression.

About two years later he wrote *The Merchant of Venice* (*c.* 1596). His serious dialogue was now better than his comic. Shylock expresses his hatred of Antonio plainly, clearly, and passionately, for Shakespeare has entered into Shylock's mind and felt his emotion:

> Signior Antonio, many a time and oft
> In the Rialto you have rated me
> About my moneys and my usances:
> Still have I borne it with a patient shrug,
> (For sufferance is the badge of all our Tribe).
> You call me misbeliever, cut-throat dog,
> And spet upon my Jewish gabardine,
> And all for use of that which is mine own.
> Well then, it now appears you need my help:
> Go to then, you come to me, and you say,
> Shylock, we would have moneys, you say so:
> You that did void your rheum upon my beard,
> And foot me as you spurn a stranger cur
> Over your threshold, moneys is your suit.
> What should I say to you? Should I not say,
> Hath a dog money? Is it possible
> A cur can lend three thousand ducats? or
> Shall I bend low, and in a bondman's key
> With bated breath, and whisp'ring humbleness,
> Say this: Fair sir, you spet on me on Wednesday last;
> You spurn'd me such a day; another time
> You call'd me dog: and for these courtesies
> I'll lend you thus much moneys.

There is still just a trace of stiffness in the rhythm, a slight but perceptible pause at the end of each line, but not a superfluous word or unnecessary metaphor. Even Portia's set speech on 'Mercy' in the Trial Scene is appropriate in the occasion and the expression.

In the first part of *Henry IV*, written perhaps nine months later, Shakespeare was first completely master of his medium. This play has a wide range of very different characters, each skilfully contrasted, but each speaks in a language which in phrase, structure, and rhythm is entirely appropriate. The most brilliant example of the contrast is in the scene where Hotspur, Glendower, Worcester, and Mortimer, compact their alliance. Shakespeare gained much by deliberate contrast. Hotspur, out of the ambition engendered in a hot head, cries out:

> By heaven methinks it were an easy leap,
> To pluck bright honour from the pale-fac'd moon,
> Or dive into the bottom of the deep,
> Where fadom-line could never touch the ground,
> And pluck up drowned honour by the locks,
> So he that doth redeem her thence might wear
> Without corrival all her dignities,
> But out upon this half-fac'd fellowship.

Falstaff, with the cynicism that comes from cold feet, grumbles:

'Tis not due yet, I would be loath to pay him before his day, what need I be so forward with him that calls not on me? Well, 'tis no matter, honour pricks me on; yea, but how if honour prick me off when I come on? how then? Can honour set to a leg? no, or an arm? no, or take away the grief of a wound? no. Honour hath no skill in surgery then? no. What is honour? a word. What is in that word honour? what is that honour? air. A trim reckoning. Who hath it? he that died a' Wednesday. Doth he feel it? no. Doth he hear it? no. 'Tis insensible then? yea, to the dead. But will it not live with the living? no. Why? detraction will not suffer it, therefore I'll none of it. Honour is a mere scutcheon, and so ends my catechism.

The contrast enhances both speakers and speeches.

Between *Henry IV* and *Hamlet* Shakespeare's technique developed rather than changed. There is not much in the dialogue or poetry of *Hamlet* that had not in some form appeared in earlier plays, but it is more competent, more supple. Each character, in long speeches or in conversation, not only speaks appropriately, but behind the words lies the whole compass of its particular personality and experience. This is seen in the less as well as the more important scenes. Thus, for instance, Hamlet having returned so dramatically to Denmark tells Horatio of his adventure on the ship which was to take him to England and to his destruction:

> Up from my cabin
> My sea-gown scarf'd about me in the dark,
> Grop'd I to find out them; had my desire,
> Finger'd their packet, and in fine, withdrew
> To mine own room again, making so bold,
> (My fears forgetting manners) to unseal
> Their grand commission, where I found Horatio,
> Oh royal knavery: an exact command,
> Larded with many several sorts of reasons;
> Importing Denmark's health, and England's too,
> With hoo, such bugs and goblins in my life,
> That on the supervise no leisure bated,
> No not to say the grinding of the axe,
> My head should be struck off.

HORATIO: Is't possible?

HAMLET: Here's the commission, read it at more leisure: But wilt thou
hear me how I did proceed?

HORATIO: I beseech you.

HAMLET: Being thus be-netted round with villains,
Or I could make a prologue to my brains,
They had begun the play. I sate me down,
Devis'd a new commission, wrote it fair,
I once did hold it as our statists do,
A baseness to write fair; and labour'd much
How to forget that learning: but sir now,
It did me yeoman's service: wilt thou know
The effects of what I wrote?

HORATIO: Ay, good my Lord.

HAMLET: An earnest conjuration from the King,
As England was his faithful tributary,
As love between them, as the palm should flourish,
As Peace should still her wheaten garland wear,
And stand a comma 'tween their amities,
And many such-like As'es of great charge,

That on the view and know of these contents,
Without debatement further, more or less,
He should the bearers put to sudden death,
Not shriving-time allow'd.

In its place this speech is simply a piece of necessary information to explain how Hamlet came back. The description is
vivid, but it is purely Hamlet's; and, moreover, it shows a little
more of Hamlet's own personality and experience: his youthful
lessons in handwriting, the touch of conscious snobbery, his sar-
donic relish of the flowery pomposities of formal correspondence,
his ruthlessness when roused.

The power of expression can be seen at its best in some of the
soliloquies in *Hamlet*. Soliloquy was an old device. In modern
stage conditions it appears artificial, but it was common and
appropriate in the intimacy of the Elizabethan playhouses.

In his earlier plays Shakespeare used soliloquy mainly for two
purposes: to give information, or as an excuse for the recitation
of a reflective poem. Thus Richard of Gloucester naïvely tells the
audience that he is not indeed what he seems to others:

I do the wrong, and first begin to brawl.
The secret mischiefs that I set abroach,
I lay unto the grievous charge of others.
Clarence, whom I indeed have cast in darkness,
I do beweep to many simple gulls,
Namely, to Derby, Hastings, Buckingham,
And tell them, 'tis the Queen, and her allies,
That stir the King against the Duke my Brother.
Now they believe it, and withal whet me,
To be reveng'd on Rivers, Dorset, Grey.
But then I sigh, and, with a piece of Scripture,
Tell them that God bids us do good for evil:
And thus I clothe my naked villainy
With odd old ends, stolen forth of holy Writ,
And seem a Saint, when most I play the devil.

Thus Richard II, alone in his prison, soliloquizes leisurely on Life and Time in a poetical 'stream of consciousness' of sixty lines.

Hamlet also soliloquizes; in general reflection, as in his broodings over suicide – 'To be or not to be' – but more often in passages which reveal also the movements of his mind, his perplexities and resolutions. At times this revelation is so subtle that Shakespeare shows not only Hamlet's mind working, but even the subconscious thought beneath. After the play-scene Claudius has rushed away, unable to conceal his guilt any longer. He tries to pray. As he is kneeling, Hamlet passes by. He is keyed up for the murder that is to revenge his father. He sees the unwitting King. He feels that the supreme moment has come. He moves towards the King:

Now might I do it pat [*drawing his sword*], now he is praying,
And now I'll do't [*approaching the King*], and so he goes to Heaven,
And so am I reveng'd: [*he poises to thrust. The supreme moment has come. He is about to take his revenge: but the word 'Heaven' echoes. It is no vengeance to send Claudius to Heaven. The moment, after all, is not fitting. He lowers his point, and steps back.*] that would be scann'd,
A villain kills my father, and for that
I his sole son, do this same villain send
To Heaven.
[*He pauses the time of four stresses in silence as the thought takes root. There comes back to his mind the murder which was to be avenged, and the Ghost's story, with its bitterest complaint 'Cut off even in the blossoms of my sin, Unhousel'd, disappointed, unaneled. No reckoning made, but sent to my account With all my imperfections on my head.' Death, here and now, would be a benefit to Claudius*]
O this is hire and salary, not revenge.
He took my father grossly, full of bread,
With all his crimes broad blown, as flush as May,
And how his audit stands, who knows, save Heaven:
But in our circumstance and course of thought

'Tis heavy with him: and am I then reveng'd,
To take him in the purging of his soul,
When he is fit and season'd for his passage?
No.
Up sword, and know thou a more horrid hent
When he is drunk asleep: or in his rage,
Or in th'incestuous pleasure of his bed,
At gaming, swearing, or about some act
That has no relish of salvation in't,
Then trip him, that his heels may kick at Heaven,
And that his soul may be as damn'd and black
As Hell, whereto it goes. [*Then with a final swirl of passion as he strides off*] My mother stays,
This physic but prolongs thy sickly days.

Othello, written some months later, is the most perfectly constructed of all Shakespeare's tragedies, and may best be used to illustrate the four different kinds of dramatic speech: lyric poetry, rhyme, blank verse, prose. All are used in *Othello* with the greatest artistry and to gain particular effects of tone, mood, and atmosphere.

In Shakespeare's plays, and in Elizabethan drama generally, the broad distinction between the use of prose and the use of blank verse is clear and simple. Prose dialogue keeps the scene down to the ordinary level of every day. The characters talk to each other with an easy naturalism. Blank verse heightens the atmosphere, giving dignity and emotion to the speakers. Certain persons naturally speak verse, others prose. Falstaff naturally speaks in prose, Hotspur in verse, whilst Prince Hal speaks prose in the company of Falstaff and verse to his father.

In *Othello* blank verse is the natural speech of Othello himself. He is a heroic and dignified person. Iago, on the other hand, is a lower character altogether. He speaks mostly in prose, but at times he breaks into verse, especially in his soliloquies when he is left to himself. Other prose characters do not. When Benedick or Falstaff come to soliloquize they speak in their natural medium, prose. But there is a distinct purpose in every change in Iago's speeches. They coincide with and express the subtle changes of his mood. Iago, the jocular, simple 'honest Iago', speaks a quick prose. But Iago feigning honest indignation or expressing real hate is an emotional being; and verse, on the Elizabethan stage, is the natural expression of emotion. At his first entry in the beginning of the play he is seething with anger because Othello has rejected him and chosen Cassio. This is the real Iago speaking from his heart. His hate jets out in spasms of indignant rhetoric:

> Despise me
> If I do not. Three Great-ones of the City
> (In personal suit to make me his Lieutenant)
> Off-capp'd to him: and by the faith of man
> I know my price, I am worth no worse a place.
> But he (as loving his own pride, and purposes)
> Evades them, with a bumbast circumstance,
> Horribly stuff'd with epithets of war,
> And in conclusion,
> Nonsuits my mediators. For certes, says he,
> I have already chose my officer. And what was he?
> Forsooth, a great arithmetician,
> One Michael Cassio, a Florentine,
> (A fellow almost damn'd in a fair wife)
> That never sat a squadron in the field,
> Nor the division of a battle knows
> More than a spinster. Unless the bookish theoric:
> Wherein the toged Consuls can propose
> As masterly as he. Mere prattle (without practice)
> Is all his soldiership. But he (Sir) had th'election;
> And I (of whom his eyes had seen the proof
> At Rhodes, at Cyprus, and on other grounds,
> Christen'd, and Heathen), must be be-leed, and calm'd
> By debitor, and creditor. This counter-caster,
> He (in good time) must his Lieutenant be,
> And I (God bless the mark) his Moorship's Ancient.

Nor does Iago regain self-control until Brabantio loses his temper. Then once more he is outwardly the mocker, speaking prose. After further, but milder expression of his anger he goes out. Next he appears in company with Othello. He is now feigning indignation, and verse is the proper medium for his speech.

In the scene in the Council Chamber Iago says nothing, but watches. At the end he is left alone with Roderigo. Again the mask is on and he speaks a flippant, supple prose until Roderigo leaves him. Then once more he is left alone and his real emotions break out in powerful passionate verse, as the idea of his plot begins to grow:

> How? How? Let's see.
> After some time, to abuse Othello's ears,
> That he is too familiar with his wife:
> He hath a person, and a smooth dispose
> To be suspected: fram'd to make women false.
> The Moor is of a free, and open nature,
> That thinks men honest, that but seem to be so,
> And will as tenderly be led by th' nose
> As asses are:

The rest of the line is silent, as the thought catches fire. Then with a little cry of triumph:

> I have't: it is engender'd: Hell, and Night,
> Must bring this monstrous birth, to the world's light.

Thus by watching the speech used by Iago we have a subtle revelation of his outward manner. With Iago prose shows that the mask is on, that he is self-controlled, 'honest', and frank. With Othello a lapse into prose denotes the opposite – a break-down of control. Othello speaks prose only when he falls into his apoplectic fit and when he sees the handkerchief in Cassio's hand.

Another very good example of the different use of prose and verse occurs in the conversation between Desdemona and Emilia towards the end of the play (IV, iii). Othello has just gone out after his vile abuse of Desdemona. Suddenly she asks:

> Dost thou in conscience think (tell me Emilia)
> That there be women do abuse their husbands
> In such gross kind?

EMILIA: There be some such, no question.

DESDEMONA: Wouldst thou do such a deed for all the world?

EMILIA: Why, would not you?

DESDEMONA: No, by this heavenly light.

EMILIA: Nor I neither, by this heavenly light:
I might do't as well i' th' dark.

DESDEMONA: Wouldst thou do such a deed for all the world?

EMILIA: The world's a huge thing:
It is a great price, for a small vice.

DESDEMONA: In troth, I think thou wouldst not.

EMILIA: In troth I think I should, and undo't when I had done. Marry, I would not do such a thing for a joint-ring, nor for measures of lawn, nor for gowns, petticoats, nor caps, nor any petty exhibition. But for all the whole world: 'uds pity, who would not make her husband a cuckold, to make him a Monarch? I should venture Purgatory for't.

Emilia for a moment is confused by Desdemona's insistence and tries to turn it off in a laugh, but as Desdemona still persists she evades her by regaining her composure in indignant protestation – in rhetorical verse – against jealous husbands:

> But I do think it is their husbands' faults
> If wives do fall: (Say, that they slack their duties,
> And pour our treasuries into foreign laps;
> Or else break out in peevish jealousies,
> Throwing restraint upon us: or say they strike us,
> Or scant our former having in despite)
> Why we have galls: and though we have some grace,
> Yet have we some revenge. Let husbands know,
> Their wives have sense like them: They see, and smell,
> And have their palates both for sweet, and sour,
> As husbands have. What is it that they do,
> When they change us for others? Is it sport?

> I think it is: and doth affection breed it?
> I think it doth. Is't frailty that thus errs?
> It is so too. And have not we affections?
> Desires for sport? and frailty, as men have?
> Then let them use us well: else let them know,
> The ills we do, their ills instruct us so.

Shakespeare uses lyric verse to create a definite atmosphere. It is always sung. There are two notable examples in *Othello*. The first is in the drinking scene, where Iago sings:

> And let me the canakin clink, clink:
> And let me the canakin clink.
> A soldier's a man: Oh, man's life's but a span,
> Why then let a soldier drink.

And:

> King Stephen was and a worthy peer,
> His breeches cost him but a crown,
> He held them sixpence all too dear,
> With that he call'd the tailor lown:
> He was a wight of high renown,
> And thou art but of low degree:
> 'Tis pride that pulls the country down,
> Then take thy auld cloak about thee.

Both songs are sung loudly and create the atmosphere of rowdy merriment which is the proper prelude and mood for Cassio's drunkenness.

The second is the Willow song. After the dreadful scene where Othello treats Desdemona as a prostitute Shakespeare wishes to prepare our mood for the murder. So Desdemona sings very softly:

> The poor soul sat sighing, by a sycamore tree.
> Sing all a green willow:
> Her hand on her bosom, her head on her knee,
> Sing willow, willow, willow.
> The fresh streams ran by her, and murmur'd her moans,

> Sing willow, willow, willow.
> Her salt tears fell from her, and soften'd the stones,
> Sing willow, willow, willow.
> Sing all a green willow must be my garland.
> Let nobody blame him, his scorn I approve.
>
> I call'd my Love false Love: but what said he then?
> Sing, willow, willow, willow.
> If I court mo women, you'll couch with mo men.

The music has the same effect as a change of light in the modern theatre.

In *Othello* there is also a notable instance of the use of rhyme. On the whole Shakespeare was sparing in the use of rhyme in his later plays. The rhymed couplet at the end of a scene was always liable to occur, but when he used rhyme within a scene it was with a definite purpose. In the Council Chamber scene, after Brabantio has been humiliated by Desdemona's unexpected declaration of her love for Othello, the Duke tries to comfort him by lapsing into proverbs, or 'sentences' as they were called:

> When remedies are past, the griefs are ended
> By seeing the worst, which late on hopes depended.
> To mourn a mischief that is past and gone,
> Is the next way to draw new mischief on.
> What cannot be preserv'd, when Fortune takes:
> Patience her injury a mock'ry makes.
> The robb'd that smiles, steals something from the thief,
> He robs himself, that spends a bootless grief.

Brabantio is irritated by these commonplaces, and retorts with a few proverbs of his own. Then, to point the contrast of mood, the Duke resumes not in blank verse, but in prose. Thus these two for the moment hold a kind of duet. As blank verse heightens speech and infuses it with emotion, so rhymed verse stiffens and gives it special emphasis. Here Shakespeare stressed the easy condolence of the man who was not touched by the sorrow of the inconsolable father. Then, as Brabantio goes out, he gives a parting message to Othello, which is both warning, prophecy, and curse:

> Look to her (Moor) if thou hast eyes to see:
> She has deceiv'd her father, and may thee.

The rhymed couplet gives just the right touch of oracular pronouncement necessary.

A few years later (1606) Shakespeare wrote *Lear* and *Macbeth*. To those who are not familiar with Shakespeare's language *Lear* is a difficult play to read because of its excessive concentration of thought. It is not so much that he uses a strange vocabulary or difficult words, as that he combines words and images to express thoughts which are in themselves almost beyond expression. The play itself was in some ways a new departure. He was concerned rather to show the significance of human conduct than to tell a dramatic story. What he wished to say could no longer be expressed in direct statement, but only by suggestion and flashes of meaning. As in his earlier plays, he was again consciously experimenting with language, but impatiently rather than joyously. He wrote speeches in great sweeps and not line by line, and even the formal pattern of five stresses was submerged in the rush of the whole. Moreover the imagery was no longer simple or direct but exceedingly complex, suggesting a dozen different ideas and associations in a sentence or two.

Edgar, disguised as the lunatic beggar, pauses in his flight to reflect on his own wretched state:

> Yet better thus, and known to be contemn'd,
> Than still contemn'd and flatter'd, to be worst:
> The lowest and most dejected thing of Fortune,
> Stands still in esperance, lives not in fear:
> The lamentable change is from the best,
> The worst returns to laughter. Welcome then,
> Thou unsubstantial air that I embrace:
> The wretch that thou hast blown unto the worst,

Owes nothing to thy blasts.

[*He sees his father, now blinded and in agony, led by an old man.*]

But who comes here? My father poorly led?
World, world, O world!
But that thy strange mutations make us hate thee,
Life would not yield to age.

Macbeth, shrinking from the murder of Duncan, soliloquizes:

If it were done, when 'tis done, then 'twere well,
It were done quickly: if th' assassination
Could trammel up the consequence, and catch
With his surcease, success: that but this blow
Might be the be-all, and the end-all. Here,
But here, upon this bank and school of time,
We'ld jump the life to come. But in these cases,
We still have judgement here, that we but teach
Bloody instructions, which being taught, return
To plague th' inventor. This even-handed Justice
Commends th' ingredients of our poison'd chalice
To our own lips. He's here in double trust;
First, as I am his kinsman, and his subject,
Strong both against the deed: then, as his host,
Who should against his murtherer shut the door,
Not bear the knife myself. Besides, this Duncan
Hath borne his faculties so meek: hath been
So clear in his great office, that his virtues
Will plead like angels, trumpet-tongu'd against
The deep damnation of his taking-off:
And Pity, like a naked new-born babe,
Striding the blast, or Heaven's cherubin, hors'd
Upon the sightless couriers of the air,
Shall blow the horrid deed in every eye,
That tears shall drown the wind. I have no spur
To prick the sides of my intent, but only
Vaulting Ambition, which o'erleaps itself,
And falls on th' other.

The imagery is too thickly clotted for paraphrase or analysis, but it expresses very adequately the turmoil of Macbeth's mind.

In *Lear* Shakespeare uses certain words and ideas in all their meanings and associations to be, as it were, the theme words of the story, two especially – *nature* and *nothing*. Lear, in his foolish optimism, regards the filial duty of affection as natural. When Cordelia offends him he casts her out as 'a wretch whom Nature is ashamed almost to acknowledge hers'. Later, when Goneril offends him, he curses her, calling on Nature to suspend her purpose: either to make Goneril childless, or, if she must have a child, that it may be 'a thwart disnatured torment to her'. Goneril and Regan he regards as 'unnatural hags', but in the end Cordelia 'redeems Nature from the general curse' that should follow her sisters' evil deeds.

Edmund the Bastard, the 'natural' son of Gloucester begotten 'in the lusty stealth of Nature', dedicates himself to her:

> Thou Nature art my Goddess, to thy Law
> My services are bound,

for Nature is the Goddess of ruthless selfishness. 'Loyal and natural boy', Gloucester calls him, with grim unconscious irony. Shakespeare uses 'nature', 'natural', 'naturally', forty-seven times in *Lear*. The words become a sinister echo throughout the play.

The word *nothing* likewise is terribly significant. Cordelia, when her turn comes to praise her father and so justify his favouritism, is tongue-tied and can utter only 'Nothing, my Lord'.

'Nothing?' echoes Lear.

'Nothing.'

'Nothing will come of nothing, speak again.'

Lear is wrong, for from this *nothing* comes everything. The word echoes in the parallel story of Gloucester, also mistaking the loyalty of his children.

'What paper were you reading?' he asks, as Edmund ostentatiously conceals the false letter which is to ruin Edgar.

He too replies, 'Nothing, my Lord', and again from 'nothing' follows everything.

Antony and Cleopatra, if the accepted date (1607) is correct, followed *Lear* by some months. It lacks the vastness of *Lear*. Shakespeare was not so consciously experimenting with this new technique of verse, but he had learnt much: he had developed new muscles. The theme did not allow for the titanic treatment of *Lear*, but the story, as Plutarch told it, called up in him an enthusiasm which he certainly had not felt in *Julius Caesar*, to which *Antony and Cleopatra* was the sequel.

The verse of *Antony and Cleopatra* has a kind of resonance which Shakespeare achieved nowhere else: a deep beauty quite its own. This quality comes out again and again in some haunting phrase or echo which exists in the sound of the words themselves, quite apart from their context:

> Oh, my oblivion is a very Antony,
> And I am all forgotten.

The exact meaning does not matter: it is a lovely sound in itself.

But poetry does not live by sound alone: it needs also perfect aptness of meaning. The finest example in the play is the description of Antony's first meeting with Cleopatra, which Shakespeare, with superb instinct, put into the mouth of cynic Enobarbus, when his friends at Rome are trying to get from him the latest Cleopatra scandal. Here Shakespeare reverted to a piece of sheer description of a kind that he had not allowed himself for years. His imagination was obviously kindled to write it by the gorgeous original in North's *Plutarch*, which was in itself a rich piece of prose. He held up the play that Enobarbus might describe the event, and in such a way that it might explain what was otherwise inexplicable, Cleopatra's power of fascinating Antony.

> I will tell you.
> The barge she sat in, like a burnish'd Throne
> Burnt on the water: the poop was beaten gold,

Purple the sails: and so perfumed that
The winds were love-sick.
With them the oars were silver,
Which to the tune of flutes kept stroke, and made
The water which they beat, to follow faster;
As amorous of their strokes. For her own person,
It beggar'd all description, she did lie
In her pavilion, cloth-of-gold, of tissue,
O'er-picturing that Venus, where we see
The fancy outwork Nature. On each side her,
Stood pretty dimpled boys, like smiling Cupids,
With divers-colour'd fans whose wind did seem,
To glow the delicate cheeks which they did cool,
And what they undid did . . .

Her gentlewomen, like the Nereides,
So many mermaids tended her i' th' eyes,
And made their bends adornings. At the helm,
A seeming mermaid steers: the silken tackle,
Swell with the touches of these flower-soft hands,
That yarely frame the office. From the barge
A strange invisible perfume hits the sense
Of the adjacent wharfs. The city cast
Her people out upon her: and Antony
Enthron'd i' the market-place, did sit alone,
Whistling to th' air: which but for vacancy,
Had gone to gaze on Cleopatra too,
And made a gap in Nature . . . .

Upon her landing, Antony sent to her,
Invited her to supper: she replied,
It should be better, he became her guest:
Which she entreated, our courteous Antony,
Whom ne'er the word of no woman heard speak,
Being barber'd ten times o'er, goes to the feast;
And for his ordinary, pays his heart,
For what his eyes eat only. . . .

> I saw her once
> Hop forty paces through the public street,
> And having lost her breath, she spoke, and panted,
> That she did make defect, perfection,
> And breathless power breathe forth.

MAECENAS: Now Antony must leave her utterly.
ENOBARBUS: Never he will not:

> Age cannot wither her, nor custom stale
> Her infinite variety: other women cloy
> The appetites they feed, but she makes hungry,
> Where most she satisfies. For vilest things
> Become themselves in her, that the holy Priests
> ·Bless her, when she is riggish.

Apart from the sheer magnificence of the speech, it was not a mere bravery – Shakespeare showing off his powers as in the Queen Mab speech in *Romeo and Juliet* or Berowne's speech in *Love's Labour's Lost*. Nor was it only an orchestral setting for Cleopatra. It is, in anticipation, part of the music of Cleopatra's death; and it comes back at the end as an echo:

> Show me my women like a Queen: go fetch
> My best attires. I am again for Cydnus,
> To meet Mark Antony.

In death as in life

> Age cannot wither her, nor custom stale
> Her infinite variety.

And indeed the poetry of the play is full of echoes:

> Let Rome in Tiber melt, and the wide arch
> Of the rang'd Empire fall: here is my space.
> Kingdoms are clay: our dungy earth alike
> Feeds beast as man; the nobleness of life
> Is to do thus: when such a mutual pair,
> And such a twain can do't, in which I bind
> On pain of punishment, the world to weet
> We stand up peerless.

Thus Antony in his moment of triumphant love. And the echo comes back later from Cleopatra, alone and deserted –

> My desolation does begin to make
> A better life: 'tis paltry to be Caesar:
> Not being Fortune, he's but Fortune's knave,
> A minister of her will: and it is great
> To do that thing that ends all other deeds,
> Which shackles accidents, and blots up change;
> Which sleeps, and never palates more the dung,
> The beggar's nurse, and Caesar's.

And again, Antony nearing his end:

> Unarm Eros, the long day's task is done,
> And we must sleep.

This is echoed by Iras to Cleopatra:

> Finish good Lady, the bright day is done,
> And we are for the dark.

It is an echo and a contrast. To Antony, the long day meant work, and then rest: to Cleopatra brilliance. She must shine or go out.

There is another note in the incomparable music of this play: its changes of mood, tone, and pace. As a modern director gains effects of change and contrast by lighting and music, so Shakespeare changed the atmosphere of his scenes by contrasts of verse, tone, and speed. Act IV, Scene xii, is a scene of battle. Antony is defeated. He enters raging against Cleopatra. She comes to him. He drives her away with fury and cursing. She reappears for a moment and runs off terrified by his wrath. And then, the fury exhausted and the passion spent, Antony returns with his servant Eros.

ANTONY: Eros, thou yet behold'st me?
EROS: Ay noble Lord.
ANTONY: Sometime we see a cloud that's dragonish,
    A vapour sometime, like a bear, or lion,

> A tower'd citadel, a pendent rock,
> A forked mountain, or blue promontory
> With trees upon't, that nod unto the world,
> And mock our eyes with air.
> Thou hast seen these signs,
> They are black Vesper's pageants.

EROS: Ay my Lord.

ANTONY: That which is now a horse, even with a thought
The rack dislimns, and makes it indistinct
As water is in water.

Antony, like the swan, is dying to slow music:

> So it must be, for now
> All length is torture: since the torch is out,
> Lie down and stray no farther. Now all labour
> Mars what it does: yea, very force entangles
> Itself with strength: seal then and all is done.

After *Coriolanus* (*c.* 1608–9) there was apparently a period of a year or more during which Shakespeare wrote nothing. Then in 1610 and 1611 he wrote *Cymbeline*, *The Winter's Tale*, and *The Tempest*. *Cymbeline* is seldom whole-heartedly admired; Dr Johnson even called it 'unresisting imbecility'; and the play is certainly overladen with familiar incidents, situations, and stock characters of the kind known as 'corny'. Yet the great set speeches – more like arias in opera – are in Shakespeare's maturest style, such as Iachimo's soliloquy in Imogen's bedchamber (II, ii, 14), or Posthumus's disgusting tirade against false wives (II, v), or Imogen's wild defence of her own honour (III, iv, 34).

Nor is the fine quality of *The Winter's Tale* always fully appreciated, but in few plays is character so sensitively expressed in dramatic speeches, especially in those of the neurotic, ill-balanced King Leontes, as, for example, when he vainly tries to persuade his minister Camillo that Hermione has committed adultery with Polixenes:

LEONTES: Is whispering nothing?
Is leaning cheek to cheek? is meeting noses?
Kissing with inside lip? stopping the career
Of laughter, with a sigh? (a note infallible
Of breaking honesty) horsing foot on foot?
Skulking in corners? wishing clocks more swift?
Hours, minutes? noon, midnight? and all eyes
Blind with the pin and web, but theirs: theirs only,
That would unseen be wicked? Is this nothing?
Why then the World, and all that's in't, is nothing,
The covering sky is nothing, Bohemia nothing,
My wife is nothing, nor nothing have these nothings,
If this be nothing.   (I, ii, 284)

In *The Tempest* he achieved what some competent critics regard as his final and greatest play. In its poetry Shakespeare reached the farthest limits possible to the English language in expression and solemn music. The thought is still packed, but no longer obscure, the verse free but perfectly controlled. The English language, unlike Latin, is not suited for precise utterance: it has too many little monosyllables which are necessary to modify its meanings. A Roman could express in a single word every mood and tense of love by conjugating '*amo*'. An Englishman must add his 'I would' or 'I might have been'. Shakespeare in *The Tempest* showed what could be done, even with English.

In the later speeches he reached his final mastery over words. The meaning is clear, the thought deep, the emotional music perfect:

> You do look, my son, in a mov'd sort,
> As if you were dismay'd: be cheerful sir,
> Our revels now are ended: these our actors
> (As I foretold you) were all spirits, and
> Are melted into air, into thin air,
> And like the baseless fabric of this vision
> The cloud-capp'd Towers, the gorgeous Palaces,
> The solemn Temples, the great Globe itself,

> Yea, all which it inherit, shall dissolve,
> And like this insubstantial pageant faded
> Leave not a rack behind: we are such stuff
> As dreams are made on; and our little life
> Is rounded with a sleep: sir, I am vex'd,
> Bear with my weakness, my old brain is troubled:
> Be not disturb'd with my infirmity,
> If you be pleas'd, retire into my cell,
> And there repose: a turn or two, I'll walk
> To still my beating mind.   (IV, i, 146)

There will doubtless come a time when this prophecy is fulfilled; but until the English language in its turn has perished, in *The Tempest* lies its greatest achievement.

9

Editing Shakespeare

When Shakespeare died in 1616 only fourteen of his plays were regularly in print, namely: *Richard III, Titus Andronicus, Love's Labour's Lost, Romeo and Juliet, A Midsummer Night's Dream, Richard the Second, Merchant of Venice, Henry IV* (Part I), *Henry IV* (Part II), *Much Ado About Nothing, Troilus and Cressida, Hamlet, Lear, Pericles. Othello* was printed in 1622, and pirated quartos of *Romeo and Juliet, Henry V, Merry Wives of Windsor,* and *Hamlet* had also appeared. The rest of his plays were first printed in 1623, when his surviving friends produced the collection in one volume known as the First Folio, which included all the plays already printed, with the exception of *Pericles* – thirty-six plays in all.

In all Shakespeare's texts there are difficulties of reading and interpretation due to errors in printing. Sometimes the misprints are obvious; sometimes phrases and sentences are quite meaningless. To make the text smooth and readable some tidying is necessary, particularly as Shakespeare apparently did not prepare his plays for printing. They were originally intended as scripts for actors and not as texts for readers. Scholars have therefore 'edited' the texts, that is, have made alterations and additions to the originals with the intention of making them more intelligible and easy for the reader.

Before the beginning of the twentieth century the original texts, Quarto or Folio, were not highly regarded. Editors believed that

Elizabethan printers were careless, ignorant men, who knew little of the refinements of literature, and could never be relied on to reproduce accurately the copy before them. Hence an edited text was preferable to an original. Modern scholars, as the result of the exact study of Elizabethan texts, have established certain principles:

(*a*) The most important authority for any text is the author's own manuscript. No play manuscript used by a printer during Shakespeare's lifetime has survived.

(*b*) The next most important text must be that printed directly from the manuscript. The earliest surviving text is therefore the most reliable, unless either a later text is based on a better original, or a later edition was revised by the author.

This sometimes happened with Shakespeare's plays. The first edition of *Hamlet* was a very bad pirated Quarto which came out in 1603; the second Quarto, dated 1604, was probably printed from Shakespeare's own manuscript, and is thus the more reliable text.

(*c*) When a play is constantly reprinted and changes of reading occur in later editions, these are usually due to later editing and therefore of little value.

(*d*) Elizabethan printing was not so haphazard as was formerly supposed; rather it differed in principle from modern usage and especially in matters of spelling, use of capitals and italic, and punctuation.

Even now, although English spelling is largely fixed, there are considerable minor differences in practice between the various printing and publishing houses. Some, for instance, refuse to allow authors to use an 's' in *civilization* or at the end of *northward*. Few authors who write in English are really expert in spelling, punctuation, or even the exact niceties of grammar, as they soon learn when a professional copy-editor has gone over their manuscript.

The history of the Elizabethan stage-play from the time when its author first sharpened his quill till it reaches a modern reprint is often complicated; and particularly in the early part of Shakespeare's career, when as yet neither actors nor dramatists regarded plays as literature. Henslowe's *Diary*, especially between the years of 1598 and 1602, gives the most valuable information. At this time Henslowe was acting as a banker to the players and made payments on their behalf to playwrights. These payments show how plays were written.

Most plays acted at Henslowe's theatres were put together by syndicates of two, three, and sometimes even five writers. Playwriting was a practical business rather than high art. In 1598, for instance, Henry Chettle collaborated in the writing of twelve plays and made alterations in three others. In 1599 Thomas Dekker wrote two plays by himself and collaborated in fourteen. Of the 280 plays mentioned by Henslowe about one in seven survives and these are mostly the work of a single author. It was only natural that an author should be more interested in his own work and so take steps to have it printed; and that the creation of a single mind should be of greater artistic value.

The *Diary* also shows that popular plays were often revised with alterations and additions. Thus Marlowe's *Tragedy of Dr Faustus*, one of the most popular Elizabethan plays, was first written in 1592. Henslowe recorded twenty-five performances between September 1594 and October 1597. The play was entered for publication on 7 January 1601. Bird and Rowley, two of Henslowe's hacks, were paid for making additions to the play on 12 November 1602. The earliest surviving quarto of the play (which is presumably not the first edition, and is probably a pirated text) is dated 1604. A fourth quarto dated 1616 has considerable alterations and additions; and in a ninth quarto of 1663 there are still further changes.

Revision and collaboration are thus present in many Elizabethan plays, and as soon as Shakespeare's plays are closely examined, it is clear that they too have sometimes been altered and revised. Collaboration in a printed play can be detected only by style, and editors are seldom agreed on matters of style. There is, however, fairly general agreement that portions of *Macbeth*, particularly the Bloody Sergeant's speech in Act I, Scene ii, and the Hecate scenes in Act III, Scene v, and Act IV, Scene i, are not by Shakespeare. Collaboration would also explain the unevenness in *King John*.

Revision is obvious in the early texts of *Hamlet*, *Romeo and Juliet*, and *Love's Labour's Lost*. In the Second Quarto of *Hamlet* there are 218 lines which do not appear in the Folio and in the Folio 85 lines which do not appear in the Quarto. In certain passages in the early Quartos of *Love's Labour's Lost* and of *Romeo and Juliet* both the original and revised version of a speech are printed. In the Second Quarto of *Romeo and Juliet* (1599), for example, the last lines of Romeo's final speech, Act v, Scene iii, are printed thus:

> Ah deare *Iuliet*
> Why art thou yet so faire? I will beleeue,
> Shall I beleeue that vnsubstantiall death is amorous,
> And that the leane abhorred monster keepes
> Thee here in darke to be his parramour?
> For feare of that I still will staie with thee,
> And neuer from this pallat of dym night
> Depart againe, come lye thou in my arme,
> Heer's to thy health, where ere thou tumblest in.
> O true Appothecarie!
> Thy drugs are quicke. Thus with a kisse I die.
> Depart againe, here, here, will I remaine,
> With wormes that are thy Chamber-maides: O here
> Will I set vp my euerlasting rest:
> And shake the yoke of inauspicious starres,
> From this world wearied flesh, eyes looke your last:
> Armes take your last embrace: And lips, O you
> The doores of breath, feale with a righteous kisse
> A dateless bargaine to ingrossing death:
> Come bitter conduct, come vnsauoury guide,

Thou desperate Pilot, now at once run on
The dashing Rocks, thy seasick weary barke:
Heeres to my Loue. O true Appothecary:
Thy drugs are quicke. Thus with a kisse I die.

At some time Shakespeare rewrote and expanded the speech; but the printer misunderstood his copy and printed both the old and the new ending. In modern texts the lines repeated have been omitted.

Every play must therefore be carefully examined by itself to see whether there are any signs of its history.

In general the history of a play manuscript is this. The author (or authors) having written the play delivered the manuscript to the company and was paid. The prompter then read it over and prepared it for performance by adding the necessary notes of the stage business and the like. Individual actors' parts were copied out with the cues; amongst the Dulwich papers there still survives Alleyn's part as Orlando in Greene's *Orlando Furioso*. The play manuscript was then sent to the Master of Revels to be censored and licensed. The play was rehearsed and acted, and the manuscript was used in the theatre as a prompt-copy. When the play had passed out of the repertory, the manuscript might be sold to a printer.

In many instances the text which reached the printer was the author's original manuscript. Towards the end of Shakespeare's career, however, when literary gentlemen liked to possess plays in their libraries, play manuscripts were copied out by professional copyists. There were good reasons for keeping the number of copies as low as possible, because as yet there was no dramatic copyright. The manuscript of a popular play might thus have been constantly altered and revised before it reached the printer, passages for omission being marked or scored through, and new additions being pasted or pinned in. It was easy for confusion and errors to arise.

All these processes can be illustrated from one of the few

manuscripts of an Elizabethan stage-play which still exists. The manuscript is in the British Museum and is known as *The Book of Sir Thomas More* – a chronicle play of the usual type, showing scenes in the life and death of More. The manuscript, which is written in seven different handwritings, has been revised and enlarged but was never printed or played in Elizabethan times. Most of the play is in the handwriting of Antony Munday, but there are additions in other handwritings which have been labelled Hands A, B, C, D and E. Of these, Hand E is Thomas Dekker's, and Hand C the Playhouse Reviser's of the Rose Theatre.

The manuscript also bears the observations and orders of Edmund Tilney, Master of Revels, who censored it heavily because of the political significance of some of the speeches in the crowd and riot scenes. He sent the manuscript back with the note 'leave out the insurrection wholly and begin with Sir Thomas More at the Mayor's sessions with a report afterwards of his good service done, as Shreve of London upon a mutiny against the Lombards, only by a short report and not otherwise at your perils'.

Such a manuscript is in itself of great interest, but the more so since Hand D, which contributed three autographed pages in a scene showing Sir Thomas More haranguing a crowd of riotous citizens, is believed to be Shakespeare's. The case was argued at length in *Shakespeare's Hand in the Play of Sir Thomas More* (1923), edited by A. W. Pollard.

The evidence for Shakespeare's authorship is of three kinds: handwriting, spelling, and poetry.

The evidence from the handwriting is the least conclusive. Very little of Shakespeare's handwriting remains. Apart from some disputable specimens, only six undoubted signatures survive and the words *By me*. There is nothing remarkable in this lack of Shakespeare's autographs. Nothing at all survives of Greene's or of Marlowe's writing. From handwriting alone it is impossible to say definitely whether Shakespeare did or did not write the Three

Pages, which, however, are not in the known handwriting of any other dramatist.

The evidence from spelling is stronger. In the good Quartos of Shakespeare's plays, which were probably set up from his own manuscript, certain unusual spellings occur. The Elizabethan compositor was free and easy with spelling, but already a conventional spelling was beginning and certain spellings are rare in printed books. The compositor would normalize an unconventional spelling; he would not make usual spelling abnormal. It is likely, therefore, that some curious spellings in the Quartos derive from Shakespeare's own manuscript. In the Three Pages certain letters are carelessly made and easily misread, especially *d* and *e* (which in Elizabethan handwriting are similar though of different size), and the 'minim' letters – *u* (which was also used for *v*), *m*, *n*, *i* (also used for *j*). Many of the misprints in the Quartos were due to confusion in the 'minim' letters; thus *five*, written *fiue*, could easily be misread as *fine* or *find* or even *fin'd*, *fume*, or *fund*. The argument from spelling, though striking, is not conclusive because as yet no one has undertaken the probably impossible task of a comprehensive study of Elizabethan spelling in general.

The literary evidence is the strongest. The crowd scenes in *Sir Thomas More* can be paralleled closely with other crowd scenes in Shakespeare's own plays: the Jack Cade scenes in *Henry VI*, the forum scene in *Julius Caesar*, and the crowd scenes in *Coriolanus*. The speech itself is similar in sentiment and rhythm to the great speech of Ulysses on 'degree' in *Troilus and Cressida*. The principal speech in the Three Pages reads in a modernized version:

> Nay, certainly you are;
> For to the King God hath His office lent
> Of dread, of justice, power and command,
> Hath bid him rule, and will'd you to obey;
> And, to add ampler majesty to this,

He hath not only lent the King his figure,
His throne and sword, but given him his own Name,
Calls him a god on earth. What do you then
Rising 'gainst him that God Himself installs
But rise 'gainst God? What do you to your souls
In doing this? O desperate as you are,
Wash your foul minds with tears, and those same hands,
That you like rebels lift against the peace,
Lift up for peace, and your unreverent knees,
Make them your feet to kneel to be forgiven!
Tell me but this: what rebel captain,
As mutinies are incident, by his name
Can still the rout? Who will obey a traitor?
Or how can well that proclamation sound,
When there is no addition but a rebel
To qualify a rebel? You'll put down strangers,
Kill them, cut their throats, possess their houses,
And lead the majesty of law in liom,
To slip him like a hound. Say now th' king
(As he is clement, if the offender mourn)
Should so much come too short of your great trespass
As but to banish you, whither would you go?
What country, by the nature of your error,
Should give you harbour? Go you to France or Flanders,
To any German province, Spain or Portugal,
Nay, anywhere that not adheres to England, –
Why, you must needs be strangers; would you be pleased
To find a nation of such barbarous temper,
That, breaking out in hideous violence,
Would not afford you an abode on earth,
Whet their detested knives against your throats,
Spurn you like dogs, and like as if God
Owed not nor made not you, that the elements
Were not all appropriate to your comforts,
But chartered unto them, what would you think
To be thus used? This is the strangers' case;
And this your momtanish inhumanity.

In the manuscript, the speech is spelt and punctuated thus:

Nay certainly you ar
for to the king god hath his offyc lent
of dread of Justyce, power and Comaund
hath bid him rule, and willd you to obay
and to add ampler matie to this
he hath not only lent the king his figure
his throne & sword, but gyven him his owne name
calls him a god on earth, what do you then
rysing gainst him that god himsealf enstalls
but ryse gainst god, what do you to your sowles
in doing this o desperat as you are.
wash your foule mynds with teares and those same hands
that you lyke rebells lyft against the peace
lift vp for peace, and your vnreuerent knees
make them your feet to kneele to be forgyven
tell me but this what rebell captaine
as mutynes ar incident, by his name
can still the rout who will obay a traytor
or howe can well that proclamation sounde
when ther is no adicion but a rebell
to quallyfy a rebell, youle put downe straingers
kill them cutt their throts possesse their howses
and leade the matie of law in liom
to slipp him lyke a hound; say nowe the king
as he is clement, yf thoffendor moorne
shoold so much com to short of your great trespas
as but to banysh you, whether woold you go.
what Country by the nature of your error
shoold gyve you harber go you to ffrance or flanders
to any Jarman province, spane or portigall
nay any where that not adheres to Jngland
why you must needs be straingers, woold you be pleasd
to find a nation of such barbarous temper
that breaking out in hiddious violence
woold not afoord you, an abode on earth

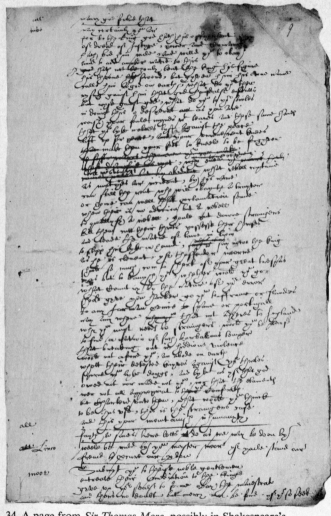

34 A page from *Sir Thomas More*, possibly in Shakespeare's handwriting

whett their detested knyves against your throtes
spurne you lyke doggs, and lyke as yf that god
owed not nor made not you, nor that the elaments
wer not all appropriate to your Comforts.
but Charterd vnto them, what woold you thinck
to be thus vsd, this is the straingers case
and this your momtanish inhumanyty.*

The case is not yet finally proved, as there are several flaws in
the original argument. The authors of *Shakespeare's Hand*
assigned the play to the year 1594 or thereabouts; but Shakespeare could not have written the passage so early, for he did not
develop so competent and fluent a style until at least five years
later. A good case has, however, been made for the year 1601. If
so, the passages which so disturbed Edmund Tilney were senti-
ments which might have been taken to refer to the rebellion of the
Earl of Essex, and the style is consistent with other plays which
Shakespeare wrote at this time.

The study of this manuscript has fostered the founding of certain principles of textual criticism: particularly that when an
editor proposes to emend a text which he suspects to be corrupt,
he must take into account the author's handwriting. If his proposed emendation is not due to a probable misreading, then it is
to be suspected. This was the principle adopted by J. Dover
Wilson in the *New Shakespeare*, which was sometimes called
'scientific bibliography'.

Actually, the principle is neither so scientific nor so reliable as it
sounds. The modern editor has not seen the original manuscript;
he can only guess what its appearance might have been. Even if it
were possible to guess what the printer saw before him in his copy,
the editor must also guess what the printer *knew*. Most men who
write fast and not too legibly produce in their manuscripts words
which are not in themselves clear; but the reader, knowing something of the matter in hand, can guess the meaning from the

* See Pl. 34 which reproduces the whole of this speech.

context. In a private letter there is usually not much difficulty. When, however, a manuscript is passed to a printer (or typist) who knows little of the subject and is not particularly interested by it, he will guess the illegible words; and his guess will depend on his education and experience. An ignorant typist, unable to read her copy, cheerfully produces nonsense; the second-class typist, not content with nonsense, makes a sense of her own. The perfect secretary makes a correct copy because she is familiar with the matter.

My own experience of typists and printers (which is now considerable) has shaken my faith in the use of handwriting as a clue to textual emendation. The most striking instance occurred in a short introduction which I wrote for an edition of John Marston's play *The Malcontent*. Contrary to usual (and wiser) practice, a manuscript copy* was sent to the printer. The proof returned with 24 errors in 2,000 words – an unusually large proportion. Some of these errors were so striking that at first glance it seemed a telling confirmation of the value of 'scientific bibliography', but on comparing the proof with the original manuscript it worked the other way. Of the 24 errors only 10 were due to misreading of the handwriting. For some the printer could not be held responsible: *Maeilente* for *Macilente*, *Lampateo* for *Lampatho*, *servants* for *seruants*. Others were possible misreadings of the script but made no sense in their context, as *make* for *unable*, *that* for *but*, *pave* for *grave*. The remainder were the printer's own unaided effort, such as *folies* for *follies*, *devision*, *reconizable*, *Johnson* for *Jonson* (twice), *John* for *Ihon* (in a quoted title page), *Parles Churchyard* for *Paul's Churchyard*. Three were particularly striking. I was made to speak of a character called *Tharsicles* in a play of *Troilus and Creosida*, and, most interesting of all, 'they [Marston's satires] pilloried many recognizable contemporaries' became (the printer's mind having strayed from Marston to a motor-cycle for two) 'they pillioned'. Of the 24 errors, less than half were due to the copy.

* In the 1930s English printers would accept handwritten copy.

These errors were a revelation of the printer's mind and standard of education. Obviously he was undereducated, unable to spell, and bored with the matter, and he never gave a thought either to context or meaning. Nor was he used to literary copy. Had he known even the names of Shakespeare's plays he would have associated *Troilus* rather with *Cressida* than with *creosote*; he would have known also that Ben's surname was spelt without an *h*.

The handwriting of an author is only one of many causes of error in the printed text, for at times printers make the oddest mistakes even when following *printed* copy. In reprints of the Penguin Shakespeares, for instance, Bully Bottom appeared in one edition as 'Billy', and 'incontinency' was watered down to 'inconsistency'. Elsewhere 'Queen Elizabeth' in printed copy re-appeared as 'Queer Elizabeth'! There is (in spite of Freud) no accounting for a large proportion of human errors.

As has been seen, only a small proportion of Elizabethan plays was ever published; most of them have perished. The players objected to the publication of plays for practical reasons, but as the standard improved, so there grew up a literary interest in plays. It set the fashion amongst literary-minded gentlemen to read plays and to collect them in their libraries. Lord Mountjoy's secretary noted one of his recreations as reading play-books. Sir John Harington in 1610 possessed 129 play-books, and he bought 90 out of 105 which were published during the years 1600–10.* It became also a practice for certain authors to make a second copy of their plays which they sold to the printers, though this was considered hardly honest.

Sometimes play manuscripts were stolen, or, if a play was particularly popular or topical, some hack would be paid to vamp up a pirated copy. The pirated texts of *Henry V*, *Hamlet*, and *The Merry Wives of Windsor* were produced in this way. Sometimes when the players were hard up they sold their play-books. After

* *The Elizabethan Stage*, iii, 183.

the dislocation caused by the plague of 1592–4, twenty-two plays were published in one year. When a play had ceased to be profitable, it was sometimes sold; and there were occasions when for some particular reason it was desirable to allow printed copies to be circulated. Thus the Lord Chamberlain's Men allowed the First Part of *Henry IV* to be published, probably to demonstrate to the world that Oldcastle's name had been changed to Falstaff.*

Although the players had no dramatic copyright in their plays, they were not without some protection. There was a printer's copyright; a printer, by the rules of the Stationers' Company, was obliged to enter (in the Stationers' Register) the title of a book which he proposed to print. The entry gave him sole right to print. In practice, however, printers were very casual in observing the regulations, and only about two-thirds of the books printed were actually entered. Books could not be entered unless the authority of the Wardens of the Stationers' Company, or the Archbishop of Canterbury, or the Bishop of London, or a member of the Privy Council, had first been secured. Players were sometimes able to prevent the unwarranted printing of their plays by appealing to their patrons. Sometimes they arranged with a printer to enter the play in the Stationers' Register and so secure copyright, but with no intention of printing it.

Most Elizabethan books were produced in one of two formats: *quarto* or *folio*. These terms describe the ways in which the pages of the book are printed and folded for binding. In a folio book the full single sheet of paper is folded once and so gives a sheet of two leaves or four pages. In the quarto book the paper is folded twice, thus producing four leaves or eight pages of print. The sheet of paper varied in size from about 11 by 16 inches to 15 by 22 inches. A quarto, before the binder cut the edges of the paper, was thus a book of approximately 5½ by 8 inches.

Quarto was the normal method of printing smaller works such as play-books. The separate quartos of Shakespeare's plays run

* See p. 110.

from the two pirated Quartos of *Henry V* and *The Merry Wives* with 56 pages each to the Second Quarto of *Hamlet* with 102 pages.

The single folding of four leaves in a quarto is called a *gathering*. To enable the printed sheets to be folded in the right way, and for each gathering to be assembled for binding in the right order, each is marked with a signature or letter printed at the bottom of the page. In most new books, the text proper commonly started with the signature B, and the gatherings are marked successively C, D, E, etc. Signature A was left for the preliminaries which are usually written last – the title-page, list of contents, dedicatory epistle, and the rest. However, if the book was a reprint, or when the printer knew that no new preliminary matter was to be added, then the first section could be gathered with a full A gathering. The signatures were repeated on the second and third leaf as B2, B3. Since many Elizabethan books are without page numberings, reference is often made to the recto (front) or verso (back) of a page. Thus a reference to the fourth page of the text of the 1604 quarto of *Hamlet* is to B2ᵛ.

In a quarto sheet the printed pages were thus arranged:

FRONT   BACK

Folio format was used for larger books. In a folio two or three single leaves were inserted one inside the other to make a gathering for binding, and the same method of signatures was used to indicate the proper arrangement. In the Shakespeare folio the gatherings are in threes – two leaves inserted into the outer leaf.

The folio pages before folding were printed thus:

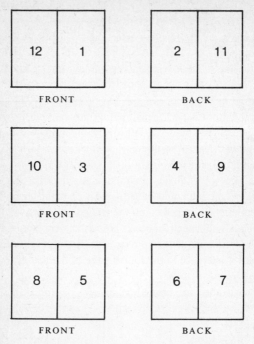

Elizabethan play texts were often carelessly printed. Some authors, such as Ben Jonson, who had a high opinion of their own works, carefully supervised the printing, but most plays show little sign of editing or preparation for the press. Spelling is more erratic than in most Elizabethan books; usually there are no place-headings at the beginnings of scenes; scenes are seldom marked; and often there is even no division into acts. Punctuation is dramatic rather than grammatical. In the Quartos the punctuation is usually much lighter than in the Folio, but is always worth careful note.* Play manuscripts were punctuated to

* See pp. 83–6.

show how the speech should be pronounced, but in most of the Folio texts it has been carefully revised.

It is surprising how varying texts can differ from each other in small particulars. The simplest way of following these variations is to give the same passage as it occurs in succeeding versions of the fencing match in *Hamlet* (v, i). The texts are: A, the corrupt First Quarto of 1603; B, the Second Quarto of 1604; C, the First Folio of 1623; D, Nicholas Rowe's edition of 1709; E, the standard Globe edition first published in 1864; F, the New Shakespeare edited by J. Dover Wilson, 1934.

A. The 'Bad' First Quarto of 1603

King   Giue them the foyles.

Ham.   I'le be your foyle *Leartes*, thefe foyles,
Haue all a laught, come on fir: *a hit*.

Lear.   No none.   *Heere they play:*

Ham.   Iudgement.

Gent.   A hit, a moft palpable hit.

Lear.   Well, come againe.   *They play againe.*

Ham.   Another. Iudgement.

Lear.   I, I grant, a tuch, a tuch.

King   Here *Hamlet*, the king doth drinke a health to thee.

Queene   Here *Hamlet*, take my napkin, wipe thy face.

King   Giue him the wine.

Ham.   Set it by, I'le haue another bowt firft,
I'le drinke anone.

Queene   Here *Hamlet*, thy mother drinkes to thee.
                          Shee drinkes.

King   Do not drinke *Gertred*: O t'is the poyfned cup!

B. The 'Good' Second Quarto of 1604

King.   Set me the ftoopes of wine vpon that table,
If *Hamlet* giue the firft or fecond hit,
Or quit in anfwere of the third exchange,
Let all the battlements their ordnance fire.
The King fhall drinke to *Hamlets* better breath,
And in the cup an Onixe fhall he throwe,

Richer then that which foure fuccefsiue Kings
In Denmarkes Crowne haue worne: giue me the cups,
And let the kettle to the trumpet fpeake,
The trumpet to the Cannoneere without,
The Cannons to the heauens, the heauen to earth,
Now the King drinkes to *Hamlet*, come beginne.   *Trumpets*
And you the Iudges beare a wary eye.   *the while.*

   Ham. Come on fir.

   Laer. Come my Lord.

   Ham. One.

   Laer. No.

   Ham. Iudgement.

   Ostrick. A hit, a very palpable hit.   *Drum, trumpets and fhot.*

   Laer. Well, againe.   *Florifh, a peece goes off.*

   King. Stay, giue me drinke, *Hamlet* this pearle is thine.
Heeres to thy health: giue him the cup.

   Ham. Ile play this bout firft, fet it by a while
Come, another hit.   What fay you?

   Laer. I doe confeft.

   King. Our fonne fhall winne.

   Quee. Hee's fat and fcant of breath.
Heere *Hamlet* take my napkin rub thy browes,
The Queene carowfes to thy fortune *Hamlet*.

   Ham. Good Madam.

   King. Gertrard doe not drinke.

   Quee. I will my Lord, I pray you pardon me.

   King. It is the poyfned cup, it is too late.

C. The First Folio of 1623

   King. Set me the Stopes of wine vpon that Table:
If *Hamlet* giue the firft, or fecond hit,
Or quit in anfwer of the third exchange,
Let all the Battlements their Ordinance fire,
The King fhal drinke to *Hamlets* better breath,
And in the Cup an vnion fhal he throw
Richer then that, which foure fucceffiue Kings
In Denmarkes Crowne haue worne.

Giue me the Cups,
And let the Kettle to the Trumpets ſpeake,
The Trumpet to the Cannoneer without,
The Cannons to the Heauens, the Heauen to Earth,
Now the King drinkes to *Hamlet*. Come, begin,
And you the Iudges beare a wary eye.

   Ham. Come on ſir.

   Laer. Come on ſir.   *They play*.

   Ham. One.

   Laer. No.

   Ham. Iudgement.

   Oſr. A hit, a very palpable hit.

   Laer. Well: againe.

   King. Stay, giue me drinke.

Hamlet, this Pearle is thine,
Here's to thy health. Giue him the cup,

                    Trumpets ſound, and ſhot goes off.

   Ham. Ile play this bout firſt, ſet by a-while.

Come: Another hit; what ſay you?

   Laer. A touch, a touch, I do confeſſe.

   King. Our Sonne ſhall win.

   Qu. He's fat, and ſcant of breath.

Heere's a Napkin, rub thy browes,
The Queene Carowſes to thy fortune, *Hamlet*.

   Ham. Good, Madam.

   King. *Gertrude*, do not drinke.

   Qu. I will my Lord;

I pray you pardon me.

   King. It is the poyſon'd Cup, it is too late.

D. Rowe's edition of 1709

   King. Set me the Stopes of Wine upon that Table:
If *Hamlet* give the firſt, or ſecond hit,
Or quit in anſwer of a third exchange,
Let all the Battlements their Ordnance fire.
The King ſhall drink to *Hamlet*'s better breath,

And in the Cup an Union ſhall he throw
Richer than that, which four ſucceſſive Kings
In *Denmark*'s Crown have worn. Give me the Cups,
And let the Kettle to the Trumpets ſpeak,
The Trupets to the Canoneer without,
The Canons to the Heav'ns, the Heav'n to Earth,
Now the King drinks to *Hamlet*. Come, begin,
And you the Judges bear a wary Eye.

   Ham. Come on, Sir.

   Laer. Come on, Sir.   *[They play*.

   Ham. One.

   Laer. No.

   Ham. Judgment.

   Oſr. A hit, a very palpable hit.

   Laer. Well —— again ——

   King. Stay, give me drink. *Hamlet*, this Pearl is thine,
Here's to thy health. Give him the Cup.

                              [Trumpet ſound, Shot goes off.

   Ham. I'll play this bout firſt, ſet it by a while.
Come —— another hit —— what ſay you?   *[They Play again*.

   Laer. A touch, a touch, I do confeſs.

   King. Our Son ſhall win.

   Queen. He's fat, and ſcant of breath.
Here's a Napkin, rub thy brows,
The Queen carouſes to thy fortune, *Hamlet*.

   Ham. Good Madam ——

   King. *Gertrude*, do not drink.

   Queen. I will, my Lord; I pray you pardon me.

   King. It is the poiſon'd Cup, it is too late.   *[Aſide*.

E. The Globe text of 1864

   King. Set me the stoups of wine upon that table.
If Hamlet give the first or second hit,
Or quit in answer of the third exchange,
Let all the battlements their ordnance fire;

The king shall drink to Hamlet's better breath;
And in the cup an union shall he throw,
Richer than that which four successive kings
In Denmark's crown have worn. Give me the cups;
And let the kettle to the trumpet speak,
The trumpet to the cannoneer without,
The cannons to the heavens, the heavens to earth,
'Now the king drinks to Hamlet.' Come, begin:
And you, the judges, bear a wary eye.

 Ham. Come on, sir.

 Laer.   Come, my lord.   [*They play.*

 Ham.   One.

 Laer.   No.

 Ham.   Judgement.

 Osr. A hit, a very palpable hit.

 Laer.   Well; again.

 King. Stay; give me drink. Hamlet, this pearl is thine;
Here's to thy health.

[*Trumpets sound, and cannon shot off within.*

            Give him the cup.

 Ham. I'll play this bout first; set it by awhile.
Come. [*They play.*] Another hit; what say you?

 Laer. A touch, a touch, I do confess.

 King. Our son shall win.

 Queen.   He's fat, and scant of breath.
Here, Hamlet, take my napkin, rub thy brows:
The queen carouses to thy fortune, Hamlet.

 Ham. Good madam!

 King.   Gertrude, do not drink.

 Queen. I will, my lord; I pray you, pardon me.

 King. [*Aside*] It is the poison'd cup: it is too late.

F. The New Shakespeare, edited by J. Dover Wilson, 1934

 King. Set me the stoups of wine upon that table.
If Hamlet give the first or second hit,
Or quit in answer of the third exchange,

Let all the battlements their ordnance fire.
The king shall drink to Hamlet's better breath,
And in the cup an union shall he throw,
Richer than that which four successive kings
In Denmark's crown have worn: give me the cups,
And let the kettle to the trumpet speak,
The trumpet to the cannoneer without,
The cannons to the heavens, the heaven to earth,
'Now the king drinks to Hamlet.' Come, begin,
And you, the judges, bear a wary eye.

> *The cups are set at his side; trumpets sound;*
> *Hamlet and Laertes take their stations*

Hamlet. Come on, sir.

Laertes. Come, my lord.

> *They play*

Hamlet. One!

Laertes. No.

Hamlet. Judgement?

Osric. A hit, a very palpable hit.

> [*they break off; the kettle-drum sounds, the trumpets*
> *blow, and a cannon-shot is heard without*

Laertes. Well, again.

King. Stay, give me drink. [*a servant fills a cup*]
  Hamlet, [*he holds up a jewel*], this pearl is thine.
Here's to thy health! [*he drinks and then seems to cast*
> *the pearl into the cup*

  Give him the cup.

Hamlet. I'll play this bout first, set it by a while.

> [*the servant sets it on a table behind him*

Come.

> *They play again*

  Another hit! What say you?

Laertes. A touch, a touch, I do confess't.

> [*they break off*

King. Our son shall win.

Queen. He's fat, and scant of breath.

Here, Hamlet, take my napkin, rub thy brows.

> [*she gives it him, and going to the table*
> *takes up his cup of wine*

The queen carouses to thy fortune, Hamlet.

Hamlet. Good madam!

King.   Gertrude, do not drink.

Queen. I will, my lord, I pray you pardon me.

> [*she drinks and offers the cup to Hamlet*

King. It is the poisoned cup, it is too late!

The textual problems of *Lear* are even more complicated.

There are three early texts – a First Quarto dated 1608, a Second Quarto dated 1608, and the Folio text of 1623. Some very clever detective work has shown that the Second Quarto, though dated 1608, was in fact a reprint of the First Quarto made in 1619; it therefore ceases to have any validity as an independent text. When the First Quarto of 1608 is set alongside the Folio text all kinds of problems arise. The Quarto is a bad text, full of mistaken readings and garbled lines, but yet – as a close comparison has shown – the Folio was seemingly printed from a copy of the Quarto most carefully revised. But again the Quarto text was not only corrected but altered for the Folio reprint. About 200 lines were cut out and about 100 new lines added. And the scholar wonders why.

If the scholar is editing the play he must then decide what version he will present to the modern reader: the Folio? the Quarto? or an amalgamation of the two – 'conflation' is the technical term? And if he is to 'conflate', what must he do when Folio and Quarto disagree in the same passage? For an example: in the opening scene, Lear turns to Cordelia for her judgement and according to the Quarto version he says:

> but now our ioy,
> Although the last, not least in our deere loue,
> What can you say to win a third, more opulent
> Then your sisters?

The Folio version reads:

> Now our Ioy,
> Although our last and least; to whose yong loue,
> The Vines of France, and Milke of Burgundie,
> Striue to be interest. What can you say, to draw
> A third, more opilent then your Sisters? speak.

Editors often choose the Quarto reading, arguing, presumably, that Shakespeare would have chosen the common, proverbial phrase 'last but not least'. Thereby they miss the whole point of the speech. Cordelia was presented as a little creature, physically overshadowed by Goneril and Regan. Lear cannot understand how so small a body should seemingly contain so brazen a heart.

In this passage it would seem that the Folio reading is the better, and it is thus easy to lay down the principle that the Folio text is to be preferred to the Quarto on the ground that it is a later revision. But yet there are also many instances when the Quarto reading is better. Is the editor then to choose by the light of his own intuition and taste? He may try to justify his choice by speculating on the shape of the letters in the original manuscript; but it is optimistic to claim that a modern editor, who has not seen the original manuscript, is less likely to err than the original reviser and compositor who had it before them.

And again, how did the First Quarto with all its imperfections come into being? What was the manuscript which the printer used? It bears traces of having been taken down at dictation; but it is too good to have been recorded by shorthand or from memory in the playhouse; compared with the 'bad Quartos' of *Henry V* or *The Merry Wives*, it is a good text.

Various guesses can be made. The first is that Shakespeare dictated it at some time when he was unable to use a pen – a sprained wrist maybe. Or, more likely, the printer, being eager to publish the play contrary to the wishes of the players, managed to borrow the playhouse copy for a short time wherein he set one or more fellow workers to take down the text in longhand at dictation. The errors are of the kind that would arise from hasty dictation uncorrected from the original.*

The text of *Lear* thus remains a fascinating problem for the detective bibliographer who can take his choice of a number of theories; but there is no final certainty in any of them; and even if there were, the study has added very little to the larger understanding of the tragedy of Lear and his three daughters. These detailed examinations of texts should, however, be of the utmost importance to those modern critics who apply the microscope to Shakespeare's poetic imagery; but they, in general, seem to be quite indifferent to that kind of scholarship.

Bibliographic study is its own reward, fascinating in itself, detective work on real problems in which the solution depends on minute, exact observation and subtle argument. But so far bibliographic study has added little to the larger understanding of Shakespeare – except for one fundamental principle which can be stated in one sentence – *for a serious study of Shakespeare's plays, the student should always go to the earliest originals, Quarto and Folio*. He will then find in the arrangement of the lines, the stage directions, even in the imperfections and inconsistencies, all kinds of subtleties which editors have obliterated, for he is only one or at most two removes from Shakespeare's own manuscript.

A modern editor is thus faced with many problems, especially in producing an edition intended for the general reader. There is so much interest in the recent work of scholars that the older 'authorized version' is no longer suitable. For the student an exact facsimile of the Quarto or Folio is the most valuable text. But the general reader is troubled by the old tall ſ which so closely resembles an *f*, and can lead to awkward mistakes, or the use of *u* for *v*, *i* for *j*, and other Elizabethan practices such as *y*ᵉ

---

* I once put this theory up to W. W. Greg who brushed it off in his usual brusque manner. Later, in 1953, the theory of longhand dictation was proposed by Alice Walker in *Textual Problems of the First Folio*.

for *the* or *y^m* for *them*. An editor must compromise both in printing and in arrangement.

In the Penguin Shakespeares the text follows the original very closely. The place-headings which were added to the beginnings of scenes by editors of the eighteenth century have been abandoned. Act and scene divisions are marked only for reference. Stage directions follow the original as closely as possible. The old punctuation has been kept unless it seems obviously impossible.

Such principles seem simple until an editor tries to carry them out. Even when there is only one original text – the Folio – there are difficult problems. In *Macbeth*, for instance, the Folio text sometimes prints short lines of verse. Editors have joined them to make complete blank-verse lines, rearranging the rest of the speech. Shakespeare sometimes began a blank-verse speech with a half-line. This irritates editors, who shift the lines up to make them look better, until they come to some line which cannot be moved. Then they leave it as a broken line and start again.

When, however, a Folio text is closely studied it is clear that much of *Macbeth* is not written in formal blank verse at all, but in a free, rhythmic verse; so also are *Antony and Cleopatra* and *Coriolanus*. But readers and even critics have not realized that Shakespeare often wrote in a free verse, because they are not accustomed to use the Folio.

For an instance. After the murder of Duncan, Lady Macbeth and her husband are surprised by the knocking; she tries to bring him to his senses. In the authorized text the speech appears:

My hands are of your colour, but I shame
To wear a heart so white – [*Knocking within.*] I hear a knocking
At the south entry: retire we to our chamber:
A little water clears us of this deed:
How easy is it, then! Your constancy
Hath left you unattended. [*Knocking within.*] Hark! more
   knocking.
Get on your night-gown, lest occasion call us,

And show us to be watchers. Be not lost
So poorly in your thoughts.

The quick, jerky utterance is much more effectively shown in
the Folio printing:

> My hands are of your colour: but I shame
> To weare a Heart so white.   *Knocke*
> I heare a knocking at the South entry:
> Retyre we to our Chamber:
> A little Water cleares us of this deed.
> How easie is it then? your Constancie
> Hath left you unattended.   *Knocke.*
> Hearke, more knocking
> Get on your Night-Gowne, least occasion call us,
> And show us to be Watchers: be not lost
> So poorely in your thoughts.

The editor's worst difficulties come when there are two or more
early texts: a Quarto and a Folio. In some instances the printer of
the Folio used a printed Quarto and made little alteration.

When problems occur, as they do frequently, an editor can only
follow his own judgement. In general he should be guided by
principles, but he soon finds that he cannot follow them con-
sistently. He can only comfort himself with the bleak thought that
he will have the same reward or punishment as all others who
write or edit books. If this work pleases, it will succeed; if not it
will disappear. Editing Shakespeare is still more of an art than a
science.

10

A Short Reading List

1 General and Reference

The most convenient and generally useful bibliography is the section given to Shakespeare in vol. 1 of the *Cambridge Bibliography of English Literature*, by F. W. Bateson, 1940; and Supplement, vol. 5, 1957. Later work is recorded in *The Year's Work in English Studies*, *The Shakespeare Survey*, and *The Shakespeare Quarterly*.

A Shakespeare Companion 1564–1964, F. E. Halliday, 1964 (Penguin Books). A dictionary of information on most matters and people that a reader might want to know. Most useful.

A New and Complete Concordance to Shakespeare, John Bartlett, 1894.

The Shakespeare Allusion Book, edited by J. J. Munro, 2 vols., 1931.

A Shakespeare Glossary, C. T. Onions, 1911.

Shakespeare's England: An Account of the Life and Manners of His Age, edited by Walter Raleigh, 2 vols., 1916. A series of studies, each written by an expert, of the many activities and branches of life in Shakespeare's England, with many illustrations.

William Shakespeare: A Study of Facts and Problems, E. K. Chambers, 2 vols., 1930. An indispensable reference book which reprints all available records and documents concerning Shakespeare.

A Companion to Shakespeare Studies, edited by Harley Granville-Barker and G. B. Harrison, 1934. An introduction to the various branches of Shakespeare study.

Narrative and Dramatic Sources of Shakespeare, Geoffrey Bullough, 1957– (6 vols. published to 1967). The complete sources and analogues for the plays.

The Elizabethan Journals, 1592–1603 and
The Jacobean Journals, 1603–1610, G. B. Harrison, 5 vols., 1928–58. A day-to-day account of those things most talked of during the years 1592–1610.

2   The Theatre

The Elizabethan Stage, E. K. Chambers, 4 vols., 1923. Indispensable for serious students.

Henslowe's Diary (2 vols.) and *Henslowe Papers*, edited by W. W. Greg, 1904–7. The most important and interesting of original documents concerning the Elizabethan playhouses and their organization. A new edition of the *Diary* and the *Papers* (in one volume) was brought out by R. A. Foakes and R. T. Rickert in 1961. This edition, though preferable for the text, lacks Greg's valuable commentary.

The Globe Playhouse, John C. Adams, 1941. An elaborate study of the Globe, though not all Adams's conclusions are accepted by modern experts.

The Globe Restored: A Study of the Elizabethan Theatre, C. Walter Hodges, 1953. Particularly useful for the many illustrations, and especially Hodges' own pictorial reconstructions of the Elizabethan stage at various periods of development.

Shakespeare's Audience, Alfred Harbage, 1941.

3 The Text

Mr William Shakespeares Comedies, Histories & Tragedies, edited by Helge Kökeritz and C. T. Prouty, 1954. A fascimile, reduced in size, of the First Folio, photographically reproduced. Most convenient for general reading, but for exact textual study an original is needed.

An Introduction to Bibliography for Literary Students, R. B. McKerrow, 1927.

Shakespeare's Fight with the Pirates, A. W. Pollard, 1919. Mainly responsible for the modern interest in textual study.

Shakespeare's Hand in the Play of 'Sir Thomas More', A. W. Pollard and others, 1923. An examination of the reasons for believing that three pages of this manuscript are in Shakespeare's handwriting.

The Editorial Problem in Shakespeare, W. W. Greg, 1942.

The Shakespeare First Folio: Its Bibliographical and Textual History, W. W. Greg, 1955.

The Cambridge Shakespeare, edited by W. G. Clark and W. A. Wright, 9 vols., 1863–4. This edition and its more popular version, the Globe Shakespeare (first published 1864), was long regarded as the 'authorized version' of Shakespeare. References to Shakespeare are still given according to the act–scene–line numbering of the Globe.

The New Variorum Shakespeare, begun by H. H. Furness in 1871 and still in progress. Each volume contains a summary and large extracts of the most important work on each play.

The New Arden Shakespeare, 1951– . Each play is given a separate volume, edited by a different editor, with introduction, text, and notes. A useful edition for the serious student.

4 Criticism

Shakespeare Criticism (from the beginning to 1850), edited by D. Nichol Smith, 1916. A large collection of the more important writings.

Shakespeare Criticism 1919–1935, edited by Anne Bradby, 1936.

Shakespeare Criticism 1935–1961, edited by A. Ridler, 1963.

Coleridge's Shakespearean Criticism, edited by T. M. Raysor, 2 vols., 1930.

Characters of Shakespeare's Plays, William Hazlitt, 1817.

Shakespere: A Critical Study of his Mind and his Art, Edward Dowden, 1875. One of the best Victorian studies.

Shakespearean Tragedy, A. C. Bradley, 1904. The culmination of the criticism of the nineteenth century; probably the most influential of all critical works on Shakespeare.

Shakespeare, W. Raleigh, 1907. A very readable introduction to Shakespeare.

Shakespeare's Workmanship, A. T. Quiller-Couch, 1918.

Prefaces to Shakespeare, Harley Granville-Barker, 4 vols., 1923–48. Discussions of *Love's Labour's Lost, Julius Caesar, King Lear, Romeo and Juliet, The Merchant of Venice, Antony and Cleopatra, Hamlet, Othello*, and *Coriolanus*. The most important critical examination of these plays – from the point of view of the director and student of the stage – yet written.

The Wheel of Fire, G. Wilson Knight, 1930. Also *The Imperial Theme, The Crown of Life*, and other works; subjective and imaginative interpretation of the ideas suggested by Shakespeare's imagery.

Shakespeare's Problem Comedies, W. W. Lawrence, 1931.

Shakespeare's Imagery and What it Tells Us, Caroline F. E. Spurgeon, 1935. One of the first and still most valuable of the detailed studies of the imagery.

The Development of Shakespeare's Imagery, W. H. Clement; in German, 1936 – translated into English, 1951. The sanest of the studies of Shakespeare's imagery.

Shakespeare and the Nature of Man, Theodore Spencer, 1943.

Shakespearian Comedy, H. B. Charlton, 1937. Followed by *Shakespearian Tragedy*, 1948.

Shakespeare, Mark van Doren, 1941. Little essays on each of the plays.

This Great Stage, R. B. Heilman, 1948. An elaborate study of the imagery of *King Lear* and a good example of its kind. Also *Magic in Web: Action and Language in Othello*, 1956.

Hamlet and Oedipus, Ernest Jones, 1949. The Freudian interpretation written by Freud's official biographer.

Shakespeare and Elizabethan Poetry, Muriel C. Bradbrook, 1951.

Shakespeare's Last Plays, E. M. W. Tillyard, 1938. Also *Shakespeare's History Plays* and *Shakespeare's Problem Plays*.

Index

More about Penguins and Pelicans

Penguinews, which appears every month, contain details of all the new books issued by Penguins as they are published. From time to time it is supplemented by *Penguins in Print*, which is a complete list of all books published by Penguins which are in print. (There are nearly three thousand of these.)

A specimen copy of *Penguinews* will be sent to you free on request, and you can become a subscriber for the price of the postage. For a year's issues (including the complete lists) please send 30p if you live in the United Kingdom, or 60p if you live elsewhere. Just write to Dept EP, Penguin Books Ltd, Harmondsworth, Middlesex, enclosing a cheque or postal order, and your name will be added to the mailing list.

Some other books published by Penguins are described on the following pages.

Note: *Penguinews* and *Penguins in Print* are not available in the U.S.A. or Canada

EDITED BY G. B. HARRISON

The Penguin Shakespeare

Two-and-a-half million copies of the Penguin Shakespeare have now been sold. Each edition contains a biography of Shakespeare, an account of the theatre for which he wrote, and a short essay on the play in question.

All's well that ends well   Antony and Cleopatra
As You Like It   The Comedy of Errors
Coriolanus   Cymbeline   Hamlet
Henry IV, Part I   Henry IV, Part II
Henry V   Henry VI   Parts One to Three
Henry VIII   Julius Caesar   King Lear
The Life and Death of King John
Love's Labour's Lost   Macbeth
Measure for Measure   The Merchant of Venice
The Merry Wives of Windsor   A Midsummer Night's Dream
Much Ado About Nothing   The Narrative Poems
Othello   Pericles   Richard II
Richard III   Romeo and Juliet
The Sonnets and A Lover's Complaint
The Taming of the Shrew   The Tempest
Timon of Athens   Titus Andronicus
Troylus and Cressida   Twelfth Night
The Two Gentlemen of Verona   The Winter's Tale

The Penguin Shakespeare is not for sale in the U.S.A., where the Pelican Shakespeare, edited by Professor Alfred Harbage, is already available.

PENGUIN SHAKESPEARE LIBRARY

Shakespeare's Comedies

Laurence Lerner

Laurence Lerner's new anthology of criticism on Shakespeare's comedies follows the pattern of his successful volume, *Shakespeare's Tragedies*. Once again he has collected together some of the best modern Shakespearean criticism, mostly written in this century, and arranged it to throw light on nine of the comedies. (He excludes the last plays and the so-called problem plays.) A general section on comedy includes passages from Ben Jonson and Meredith.

Excellence, not inaccessibility, has been the criterion for a book which is designed to interest the general reader of Shakespeare as much as the student of literature. The contributors, therefore, run from Shaw, Freud, and Quiller-Couch to Granville-Barker, Middleton Murry, Auden, and Empson, and on to more recent critics such as C. L. Barber, Anne Righter, and Cyrus Hoy.

PENGUIN SHAKESPEARE LIBRARY

Shakespeare and the idea of the play

Anne Righter

What was Shakespeare's attitude towards the theatre? How far did he share contemporary assumptions about the stage, and in what respects was he an experimental dramatist?

In this book Anne Righter discusses Shakespeare's plays in relation to sixteenth-century dramatic ideas, and considers how the relationship between actors and audience changed after the medieval plays. Shakespeare's plays are covered chronologically under such topics as the play metaphor and its proliferation into figures of shadows and dreams, the player king, the plot devices of deceit and disguise, and the use of the actor image in the major tragedies. Mrs Righter argues that Shakespeare finally developed a strong revulsion from the theatre which is reflected in the imagery of his last plays.

'I have never before read a book (is there one?) which invited me to consider Shakespeare's achievement from this point of view. The result is one of those extremely rare critical works that change one's attitude towards the subject.' – John Wain in the *Observer*

Elizabethan Love Stories

Edited by T. J. B. Spencer

The texts of eight love stories known to Shakespeare and used in the plots of his plays:

Giletta of Narbona – *All's Well That Ends Well*
Romeo and Julietta – *Romeo and Juliet*
Apolonius and Silla – *Twelfth Night*
Promos and Cassandra – *Measure for Measure*
Felix and Felismena – *The Two Gentlemen of Verona*
Bernardo and Genevra – *Cymbeline*
Giannetto of Venice and the Lady of Belmont – *The Merchant of Venice*
Disdemona and the Moorish Captain – *Othello*

Professor Spencer's introduction and explanation of the links between these stories and Shakespeare's plays, together with the glossary and bibliography, make this an ideal volume to assist the reader to make his own study of Shakespeare's methods in constructing his plots.

Shakespeare's Plutarch

Edited by T. J. B. Spencer

Sir Thomas North's translation of Plutarch's *Lives of the Noble Grecians and Romans* was one of the great achievements of Elizabethan literature. Plutarch's understanding of character and North's vigorous use of the English language attract the modern reader as they seem to have attracted Shakespeare.

Shakespeare showed unusual respect for the language and style of North when he was writing his three Roman plays. In this volume four lives from North's Plutarch – those of Julius Caesar, Brutus, Marcus Antonius, and Coriolanus – have been collated with extracts from the three plays *Julius Caesar*, *Antony and Cleopatra*, and *Coriolanus*. In this way the reader can see almost at a glance how and why Shakespeare adapted his source.

PENGUIN SHAKESPEARE LIBRARY

Shakespeare's Tragedies
An Anthology of Modern Criticism

Edited by Laurence Lerner

Shakespeare's tragedies have always been fertile acres for comment and criticism. The same dramas which inspired a Keats to write poetry appealed to A. C. Bradley – or to Ernest Jones, the psycho-analyst – as studies of character; and where the New Criticism has been principally interested in language and imagery, other critics in America have seen the plays as superb examples of plot and structure. Most of Aristotle's elements of tragedy have found their backers, and – as the editor points out in his introduction – these varying approaches to Shakespeare are by no means incompatible.

In what *The Times Literary Supplement* described as an 'excellent collection' Laurence Lerner has assembled the best examples of the modern schools of criticism and arranged them according to the plays they deal with. With its 'Suggestions for Further Reading' and the general sections on tragedy, this is a book which will stimulate the serious reader and do much to illuminate Shakespearian drama.